TABLE OF CONTENTS

"Thanks to everyone in iCodeNext who helped me so much for their encouragement and support. Special thanks to my mum, the most encouraging person I know, and my dad, who has helped me throughout the book. Thank you to MIT Scratch tool through which I have learnt coding and has given me the inspiration to develop projects for children so they can learn programming."

How to use this book

In this book, we teach the Scratch blocks used in coding. We will give you steps on developing the code for your brand new projects. Each project will commence in the book with a header in a large font, and beneath that there will be a picture of the completed project, to give you an idea of what the project should look like when it is finished.

For example:

> This is the title of the project

PROJECT EXAMPLE 1: STAR BOX

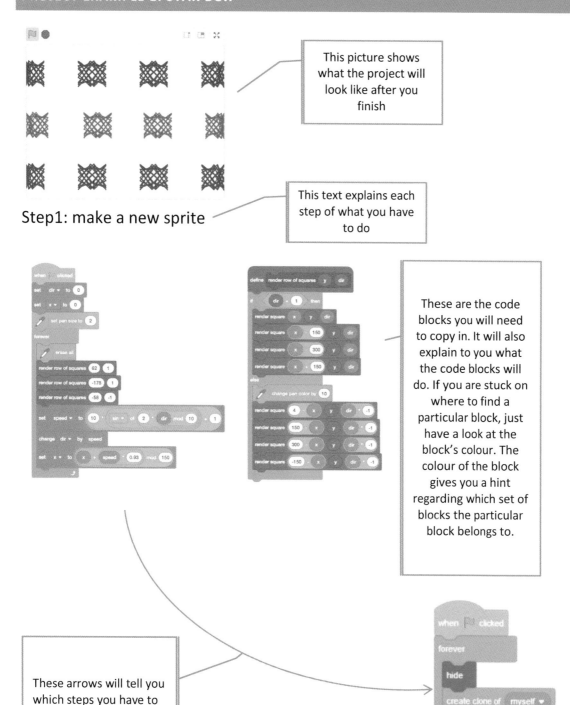

> This picture shows what the project will look like after you finish

Step1: make a new sprite

> This text explains each step of what you have to do

> These are the code blocks you will need to copy in. It will also explain to you what the code blocks will do. If you are stuck on where to find a particular block, just have a look at the block's colour. The colour of the block gives you a hint regarding which set of blocks the particular block belongs to.

> These arrows will tell you which steps you have to go to next (Follow the arrow after you have completed a particular step)

5

There are many types of games in this world. They come in different shapes and sizes. Many people like racing games, but other people prefer platform games. What's your favourite game?

Fighting

A fighting game is a great way to challenge your friends.

Music/dance

Now you don't need an instrument to play music. You can use your computer. You can make music and songs, and you can dance to them

Puzzle

Making games which require you to use your brain is a great idea. It helps you to learn in a fun, interactive way, using the computer, rather than just using a pen or pencil and paper.

Racing

Racing games use speed. By learning to use the variables and the blocks in Scratch you can make a racing project.

Sport

Sport games can be very enjoyable and innovative. You can play the same sports you do outside, but you can move around using the arrow keys on your computer.

Story

Children conjure up many stories in their minds. They can express themselves by putting their stories into code

Scratch is one of the most widely used block coding tools in the world. With Scratch, you can program your own interactive stories, games, and animations and share your creations with others in the online community. Scratch helps young people learn to think creatively and to work collaboratively. After finishing the projects in this book, you will have learnt.

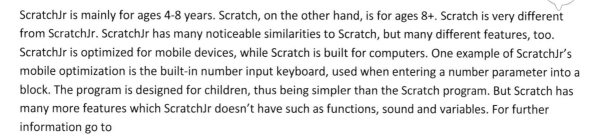

- Understanding programming concepts
- Making intermediate level projects
- What are the various block commands?
- Where are the blocks, sprites, library, music etc. found in Scratch?

WHICH IS BETTER? SCRATCHJR, OR SCRATCH?

ScratchJr is mainly for ages 4-8 years. Scratch, on the other hand, is for ages 8+. Scratch is very different from ScratchJr. ScratchJr has many noticeable similarities to Scratch, but many different features, too. ScratchJr is optimized for mobile devices, while Scratch is built for computers. One example of ScratchJr's mobile optimization is the built-in number input keyboard, used when entering a number parameter into a block. The program is designed for children, thus being simpler than the Scratch program. But Scratch has many more features which ScratchJr doesn't have such as functions, sound and variables. For further information go to

https://en.scratch-wiki.info/wiki/ScratchJr - ScratchJr

https://en.scratch-wiki.info/wiki/Scratch - Scratch

WHAT HAS CHANGED FROM SCRATCH 2.0 TO SCRATCH 3.0?

Scratch 3.0 is a complete redesign of Scratch 2.0. The blocks are bigger and brighter. It is now easier to locate where the various Scratch components are. In version 3.0 there are more extensions such as Lego Mindstorms EV3, Lego Education WeDo 2.0, Text to Speech, Translation, Micro: bit, Makey Makey and GoDirect Force & Acceleration.

WHAT IS IN THIS BOOK?

In this book, we will be talking about the blocks used in Scratch, and we will be teaching you how to make Scratch projects. You will be developing 30 Intermediate Scratch projects in this book. Let's start off with the blocks in Scratch. In Scratch, you use blocks. You might have seen people doing coding by typing text. When you are typing in the code, it is called text coding.

WHAT PLATFORM DOES SCRATCH RUN ON?

According to the Scratch Wiki, Scratch 3.0 is not based on Scratch 2.0 - rather, it is a completely new HTML5 based code-base made up of multiple components such as "Scratch-GUI", the main part of the program, and "Scratch-VM", which interprets code.

WHAT ARE FUNCTIONS?

In Scratch, functions are a way to group multiple (perhaps tens or hundreds) code blocks into a single named block, which can then be reused again and again by just including that single named block

WHERE DID CODING COME FROM?

In 1842, Ada Lovelace was the first person to write a computer program. She was also the first one to publish a program using an algorithm. However, the computer she wrote the program for, Charles Babbage's Analytical Engine, only existed in their imaginations. It was never actually built. However, some experts believe that Ada Lovelace's program may well have worked successfully were the analytical engine ever actually built.

In 1936 the first real computer was made by German Konrad Zuse and named the Z1. You couldn't write any modern code on it, and it never worked well. A later Zuse creation, the Z3, was demonstrated to the public, and still, later, the Z4 became the world's first commercial computer. A fully working version of the Z1 was reproduced in 1989.

Modern code is just like a language, but for computers. English, Hindi, French and more, are languages used by people. People who speak English, but don't know Hindi, can't understand what a person speaking Hindi is saying. The same is true with computers. When you type "abc" into the computer, the computer itself doesn't understand what you put in. So how can we make a computer understand us?

In 1952 Grace Hopper developed a compiler, which is a special program which translates our typed input into the binary language used by the computer. Grace Hopper's compiler was called the A-0 System. After making the A-0 System, she and her group made the A-1 and A-2, Improvements over the original version. The A-2 Compiler was the first compiler to be used for programming.

HOW WAS THE FIRST CODE WRITTEN?

When the first code was developed, it was written in raw machine code, using binary digits. The problem with the raw machine coding was that it was really slow to write, and it required very hard work. Nowadays we can just take our laptops anywhere. We can sit down at a coffee shop, and we just open our laptop and start coding. In those earlier times, the computers were so big that they required many people to move them. In fact, the old computers were hardly ever moved. Who was the first software developer? Arguably, the first software developer was Alan Turing. You should thank all these people, because without them you wouldn't be able to watch YouTube late at night or watch Netflix while sitting on your couch.

WHAT IS THE OLDEST COMPUTER LANGUAGE?

The oldest computer language was devised in 1958. It was called Algol. It was created by a committee of twelve people. Algol is one of a family of imperative computer programming languages, originally developed around the mid 1950's. Many other programming languages were influenced by Algol. Algol uses text coding almost exclusively.

First Computer ever made

Concept	Example	Scratch Code
Sequence - Order of events	You wake up in the morning, then you brush your teeth, then you get dressed for school, pack your bag, then eat your breakfast, then go to school. This is an example of how we do tasks step by step in a particular order, which is called a sequence.	
Conditions- Define Rules	Have your parents ever said, "if you finish your homework, then you can play"? I have. Conditions contain the words IF and THEN. For example, IF it is raining, THEN you have to wear a raincoat. IF, THEN and ELSE form conditional statements.	
Bugs and debugging	You all know what a bug is, right? The little insect that crawls in your house. Did you know that we also use the words bugs and debugging in coding? A bug means there is a problem with your program or the code in your project. If you have developed your code incorrectly, then your project won't work. We say then that there is a bug in your program. When you fix your code, that's called debugging.	
Loops – To repeat a task one or more times	You might be asking: why do we need loops when we can write the same piece of code five times over? Instead of writing the same piece of code five times, again and again, we can write it just once inside a loop block, and then the loop block will execute the code in the loop five times, or any number of times we specify. In Scratch, there are two types of loops, Open and Closed. The forever loop is an open loop, because no condition exists to make the loop stop. Repeat is a closed loop because when using it we have to mention how many times we want it to run. With a while block, we only run the code inside the loop while the related condition is true.	
Variables - Name of a storage location where we can store information	In many games, we have a 'score' as a variable, like a box to store the information about a player's score.	
Data types of variables	If you want to make rules using variables then you need to declare data types. String – You can store letters of the alphabets, numbers, and special characters. Integer – You can store only whole positive and negative numbers. Boolean – You can store only two values, such as true and false.	Scratch blocks to declare numbers, Add an input number or text / Add an input boolean / Add a label
Algorithms	A process or set of rules to be followed in calculations or problem-solving operations, especially by a computer.	
Functions	A function is a type of procedure or routine. Some programming languages make a distinction between a function, which returns a value, and a procedure, which performs some operation but does not return a value. In Scratch, we use My Blocks for functions.	

9

There is an online version of Scratch, and an offline version also. They are both very similar, but the offline version of Scratch allows you to work on Scratch without an internet connection. To use the offline version of Scratch, you first have to download it. The only significant differences between the offline and online versions of Scratch are that you can't share projects, you can't create an account, and you can't see other people's projects or accounts. If you want to work online, which is recommended, then skip to page 18, otherwise follow the steps below.

To download scratch, follow the steps below,

Step 1: Go to the Scratch using your web browser- https://scratch.mit.edu/

Step 2: Scroll down to the bottom of the page to where there is it says **Support**

Step 3: Click the link which says "Offline Editor"

Step 4: After you click it should bring you to this page

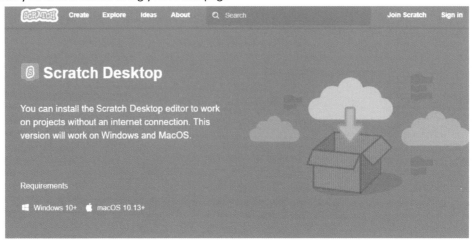

Step 5: If you have a Windows Computer, click the "Windows" button, but if you have a Mac, click the "macOS" button

Step 6: Scroll down a bit down to where is says "Install Scratch desktop" click a Download option (from Microsoft, or Direct download), and save it into your Desktop (you can save it anywhere you want, but Desktop is recommended).

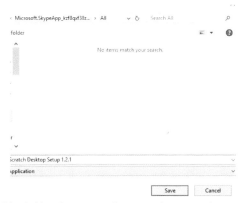

If you have a Mac then it should look like this. Drag the scratch 3.0 Desktop icon to the Application area

After you download the application, and when you open it, it should look like this

11

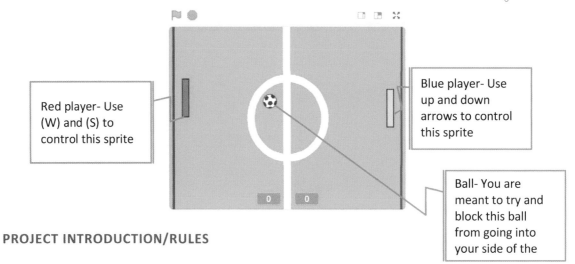

Red player- Use (W) and (S) to control this sprite

Blue player- Use up and down arrows to control this sprite

Ball- You are meant to try and block this ball from going into your side of the

PROJECT INTRODUCTION/RULES

In this game you have to try to stop the ball from going to the edge of your area. If it does the other side gains one point. This game is played like ping pong, but it looks more like soccer.

Sprite	Backdrops
⚽	O
▮	Blue win
▯	Red win

Step1: delete the cat sprite and make these three backdrops:

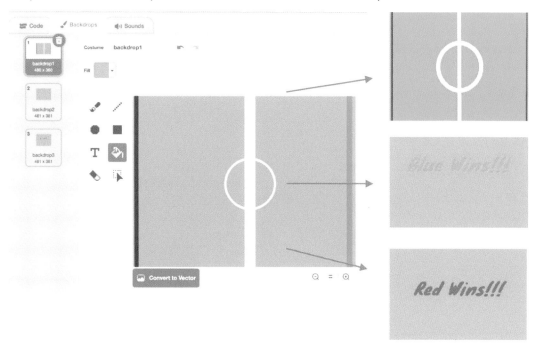

Step2: Enter the code for the Soccer ball

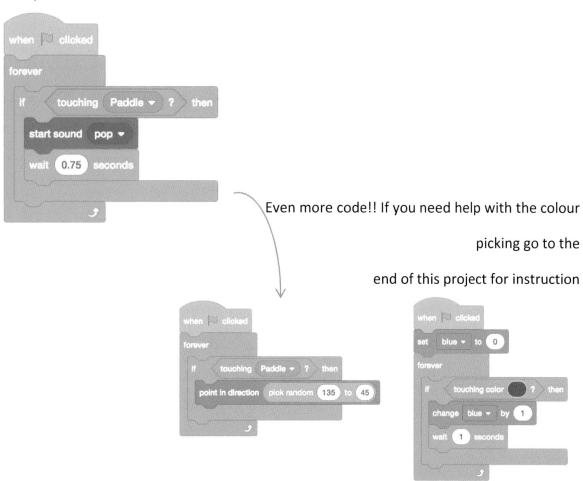

Even more code!! If you need help with the colour

picking go to the

end of this project for instruction

Even more codes!!!

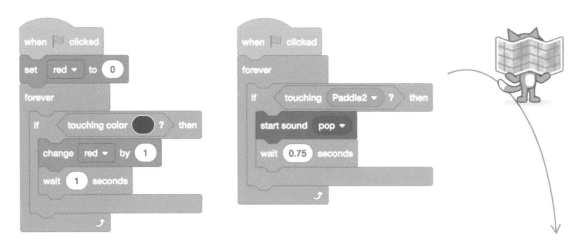

Even more code!!!

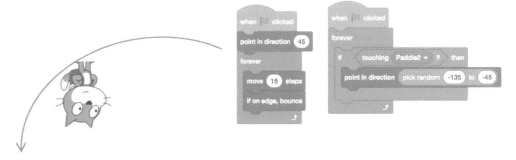

Step3: Enter the code for the red paddle

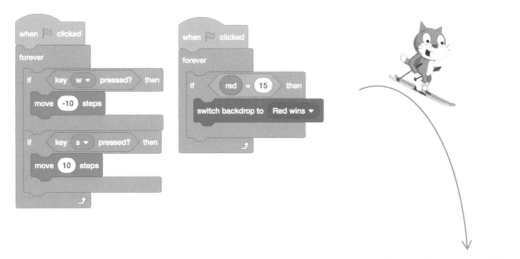

Step 4: Enter the code for the blue paddle

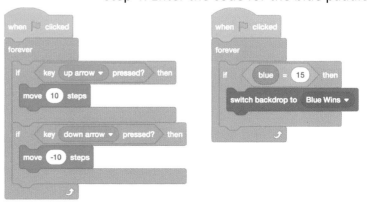

14

If you need help getting the correct colours to use in the Sensing blocks, then these are the steps to take

Step 1: Click the circle

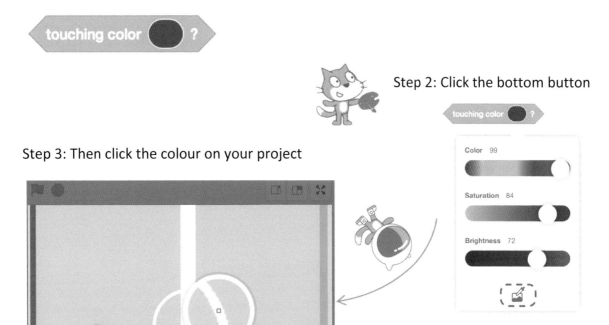

Step 2: Click the bottom button

Step 3: Then click the colour on your project

Now you have finished making your first game!!! The Soccer Block game. Rename your project and save it if you wish to keep it.

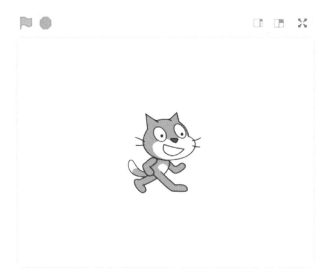

PROJECT INTRODUCTION/RULES

In this project you can make the sprite grow and make it smaller.

This is important because when you start a game you can be more creative by making the button bigger when mouse on button and smaller when it is taken of

Sprites	Backdrop
Cat	Paint the backdrop white

Step1: Don't delete your cat but if you want another sprite, then you can change from the cat to that sprite.

Step2: Enter the code for the cat

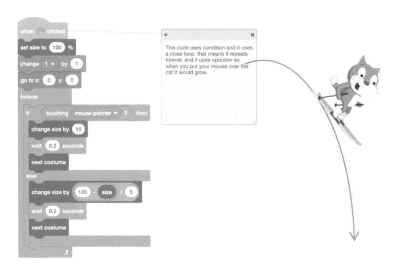

If you need help on how to connect the Operators, follow along here:

First, get your divide block out

Second, get your minus block out

Third, get your size block out and connect it to the number 100 on your minus block

Fourth, connect the minus block to the divide block

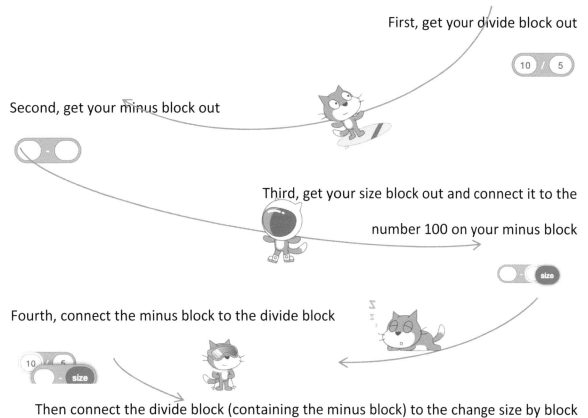

Then connect the divide block (containing the minus block) to the change size by block

After you have entered the code for the cat, rename and save your project. You have now completed the Cat Grows project.

PROJECT INTRODUCTION/RULES

This is going to be your first time making a text to speech project about food. You have to pick the good foods, and avoid the bad. If you pick the good foods you get 1 point. If you pick the bad foods you lose a point.

Sprite	Backdrops
Cheesy Puffs	Paint the backdrop white
Orange	
Fruit Salad	
Donut	
Watermelon	
Giga	

Step 1: Enter the code for the CheesyPuffs

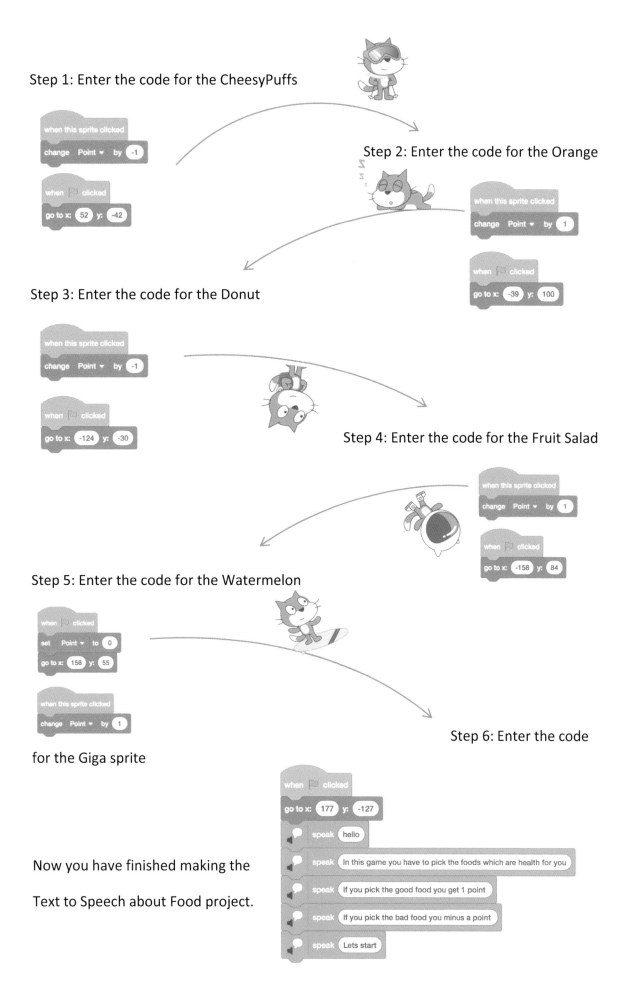

```
when this sprite clicked
change  Point ▾  by  -1

when ⚑ clicked
go to x: 52  y: -42
```

Step 2: Enter the code for the Orange

```
when this sprite clicked
change  Point ▾  by  1

when ⚑ clicked
go to x: -39  y: 100
```

Step 3: Enter the code for the Donut

```
when this sprite clicked
change  Point ▾  by  -1

when ⚑ clicked
go to x: -124  y: -30
```

Step 4: Enter the code for the Fruit Salad

```
when this sprite clicked
change  Point ▾  by  1

when ⚑ clicked
go to x: -158  y: 84
```

Step 5: Enter the code for the Watermelon

```
when ⚑ clicked
set  Point ▾  to  0
go to x: 158  y: 55

when this sprite clicked
change  Point ▾  by  1
```

Step 6: Enter the code for the Giga sprite

Now you have finished making the

Text to Speech about Food project.

```
when ⚑ clicked
go to x: 177  y: -127
💬 speak  hello
💬 speak  In this game you have to pick the foods which are health for you
💬 speak  If you pick the good food you get 1 point
💬 speak  If you pick the bad food you minus a point
💬 speak  Lets start
```

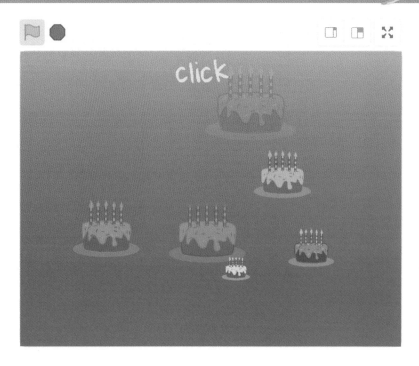

PROJECT INTRODUCTION/RULES

In this project you will be clicking on the project and making cool noises. Thanks to @mers and @Scratchteam for the Project

Sprites	Backdrop
Cake Costumes: 2	click

Step1: get a new sprite

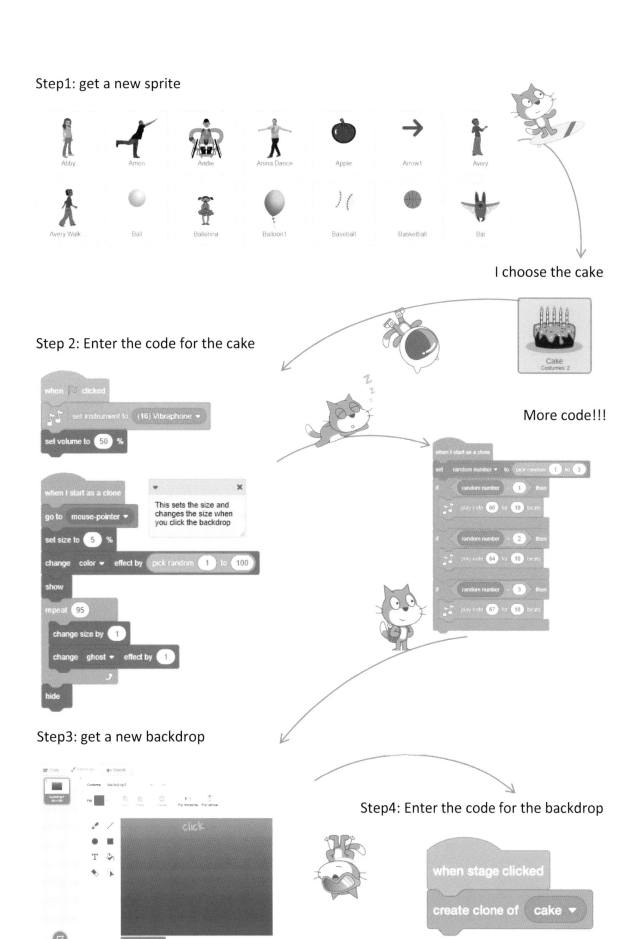

I choose the cake

Step 2: Enter the code for the cake

More code!!!

This sets the size and changes the size when you click the backdrop

Step3: get a new backdrop

Step4: Enter the code for the backdrop

Now you have finished making the Chimes project.

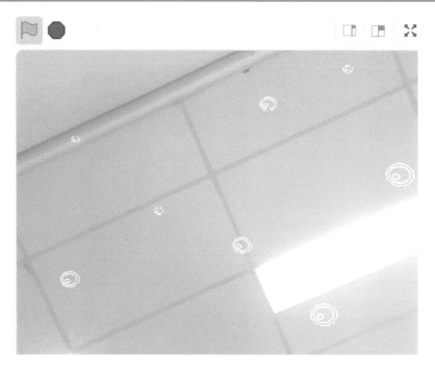

PROJECT INTRODUCTION/RULES

In this project you have to pop the bubbles by using your head and hands. They used video camera to do this project. You can only do this project if you have a camera on your laptop, or a webcam.

Sprite	Backdrop
	There is no backdrop in this project. You will be able to see yourself as a backdrop

Step1: make a bubble sprite

Step2: enter the code for the bubble. You will need to add the Video Motion extension and allow permission for the project to use it when requested by your browser. Remember that you also have to add the video Extension

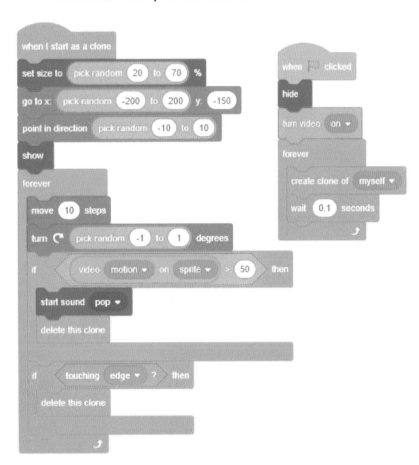

YOU CAN ONLY DO THIS PROJECT IF YOU HAVE A LAPTOP CAMERA OR A WEB CAM.

Now you have finished making the Bubble Pop project.

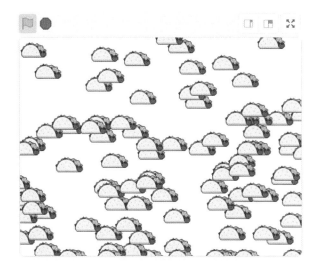

PROJECT INTRODUCTION/RULES

This is a project where we use cloning. Cloning is used when you want to create many duplicate sprites from a single sprite. If you are making a project which needs water to fall from the sky, then you can use the exact same code as this project!

Sprites	Backdrops
Taco Costumes: 2	Paint the backdrop white

Step1: Delete the cat sprite, and get a new sprite from the library called Taco

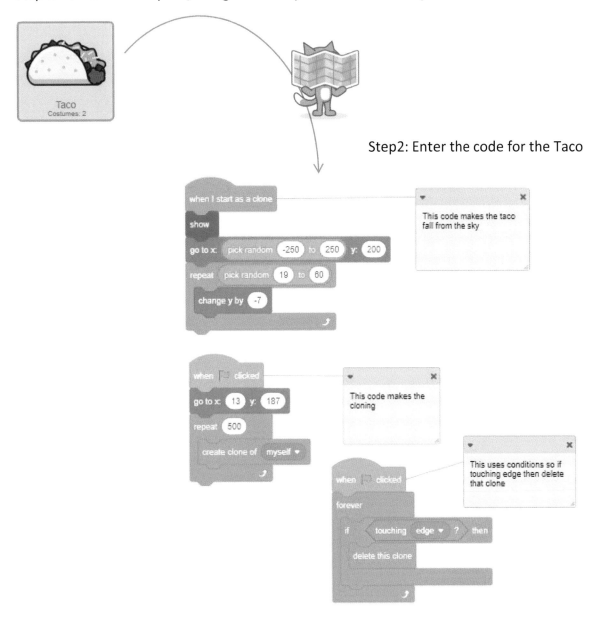

Step2: Enter the code for the Taco

You have finished making the Raining Tacos project.

You can even change the sprite if you want.

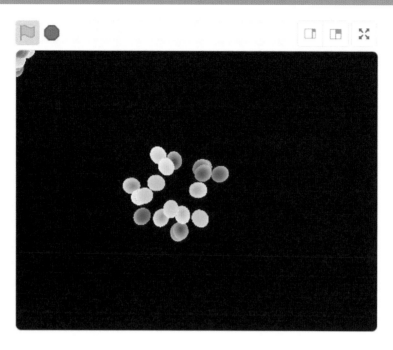

PROJECT INTRODUCTION/RULES

In this project you would be able to see circles changing colours and then fading away. You have to use your mouse pointer to make the dots follow you.

Sprite	Backdrop
●	Paint the backdrop black

Step1: Delete the cat, and make a new sprite

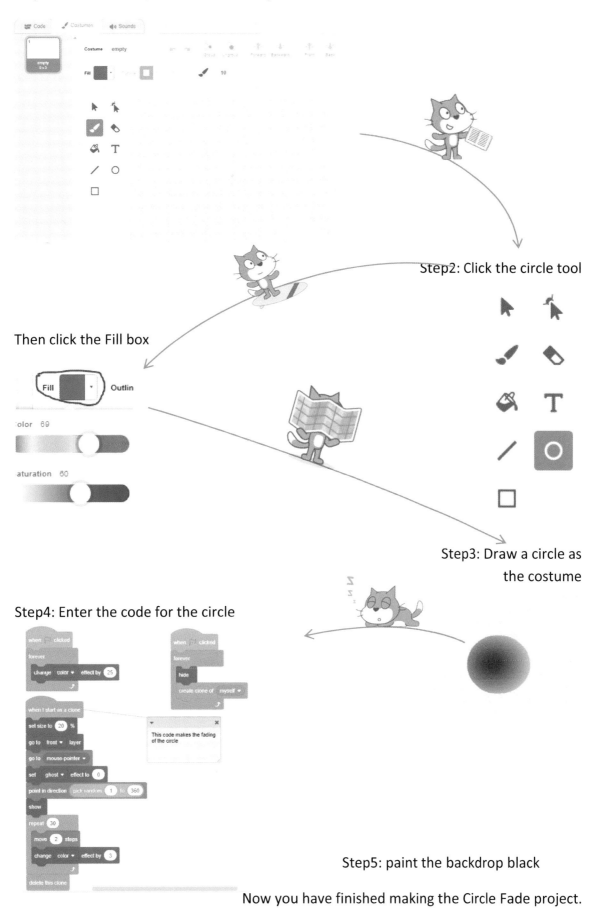

Step2: Click the circle tool

Then click the Fill box

Step3: Draw a circle as the costume

Step4: Enter the code for the circle

This code makes the fading of the circle

Step5: paint the backdrop black

Now you have finished making the Circle Fade project.

PROJECT INTRODUCTION/RULES

This project is an art project where you would see a flower being made by the pen block and motion block. You don't have to press any keys.

Sprite	Backdrop
	Paint the backdrop white

Step1: make an oval. Use multiple colours for the best effect.

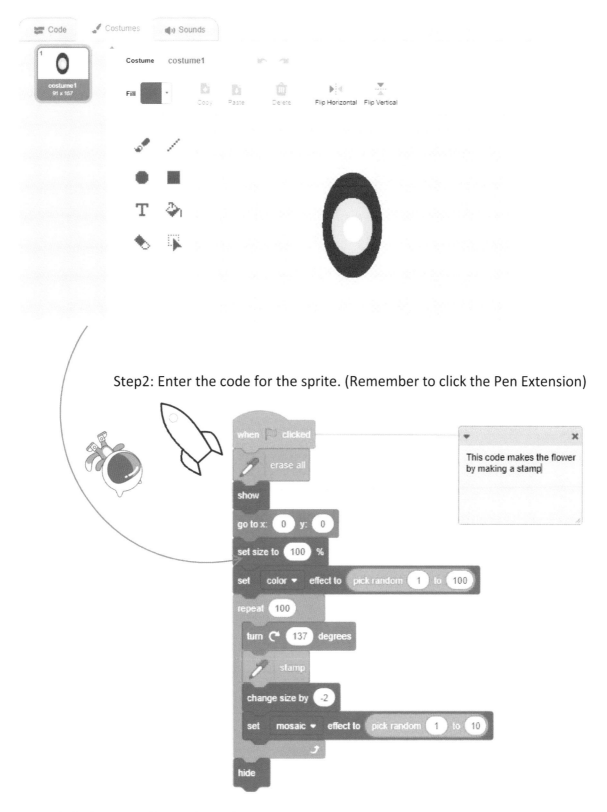

Step2: Enter the code for the sprite. (Remember to click the Pen Extension)

This code makes the flower by making a stamp

Now click the green flag and see the magic.

You have finished making the Flower Generator project.

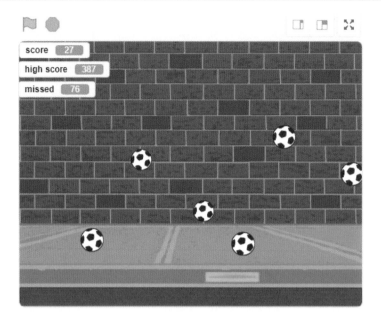

PROJECT INTRODUCTION/RULES

This project is a popular game in Scratch. In this game, you have to try to save as many soccer balls as you can by using the right and left arrow keys to move the green paddle. If you can make the green paddle hits a soccer ball you will gain a point, but if you miss the soccer ball you will lose a point.

Sprite	Backdrop
Ball-Soccer	Wall 1
Paddle	

Step1: Delete the cat. get a ball sprite

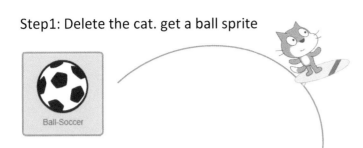

Step2: Enter the code for the ball

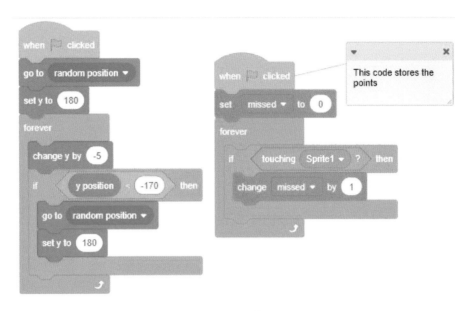

Even more code!!!

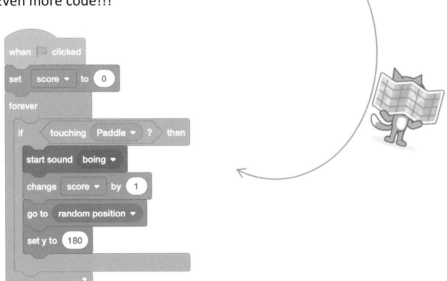

Step3: duplicate the ball five times to create five more balls

Now you have six balls

Step4: Make a new sprite

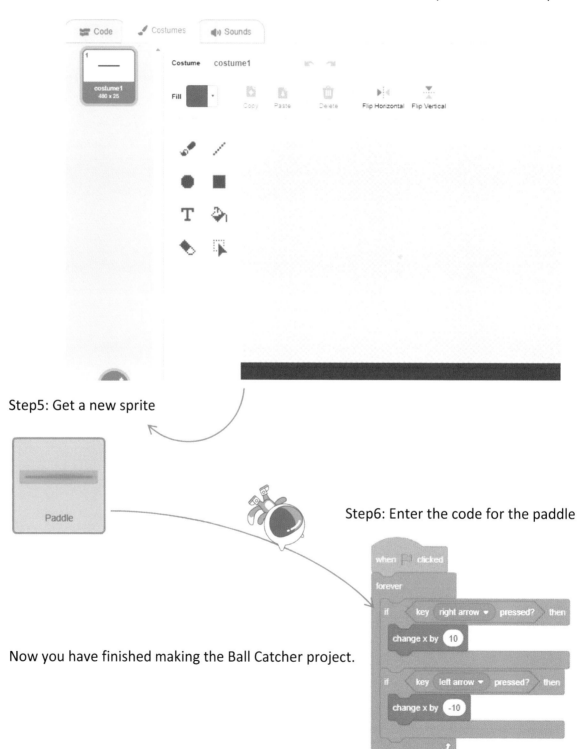

Step5: Get a new sprite

Step6: Enter the code for the paddle

Now you have finished making the Ball Catcher project.

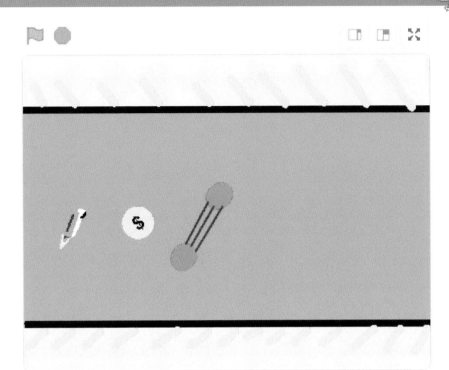

PROJECT INTRODUCTION/RULES

This project is a very popular game. You might have played this game on some of your devices. You are the human who is trying to avoid the electric balls while trying to collect the coins. If you don't press any keys you will fall down but if you press any keys you will start flying.

Sprite	Backdrop
PLAY	
$	

Step1: delete the cat and make a new sprite and call it Sprite 2.

Step2: Enter the code for the human

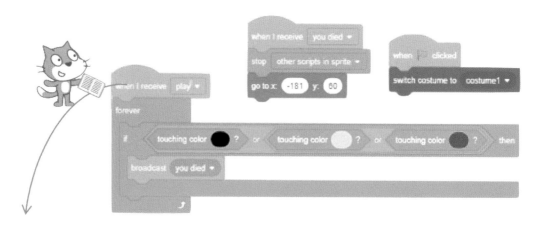

There is even more code

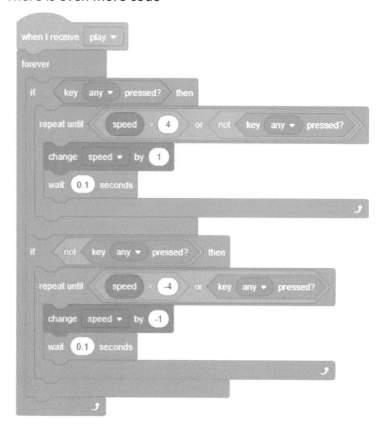

Even more code!!!

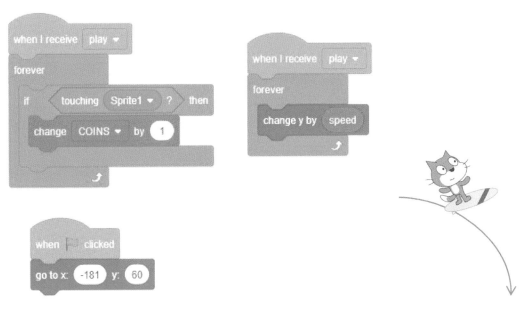

Step 3: make a new sprite and name it jetpack. For this you have to make 2 costumes, which we will eventually name to costume7 and costume8.

Make Costume 1 for jetpack

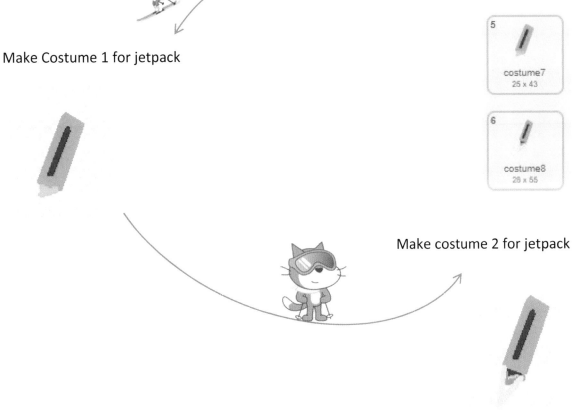

Make costume 2 for jetpack

Remember to also add the flame under the jetpack for costume 2

Step4: you have to change the label on the top from costume 1 to costume 7.

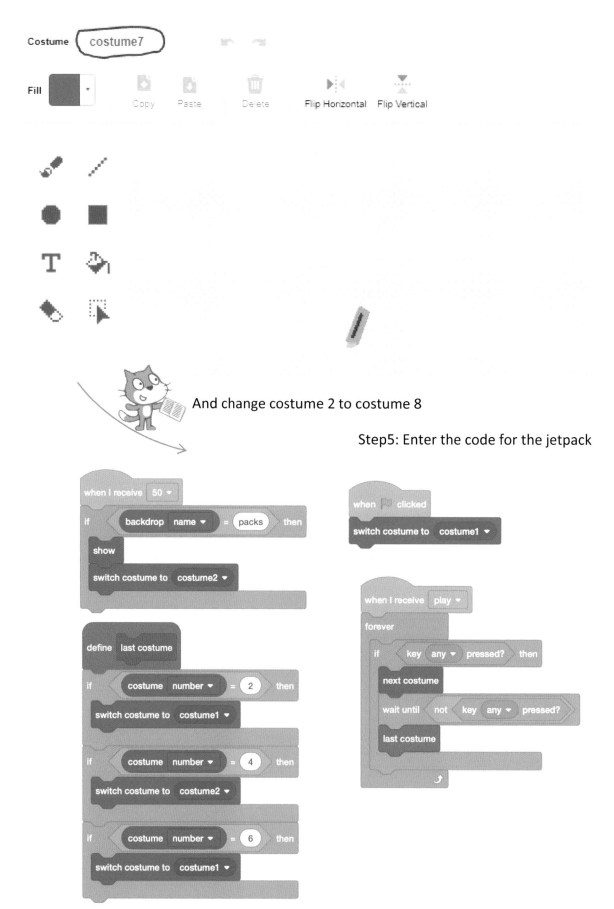

And change costume 2 to costume 8

Step5: Enter the code for the jetpack

There are even more codes

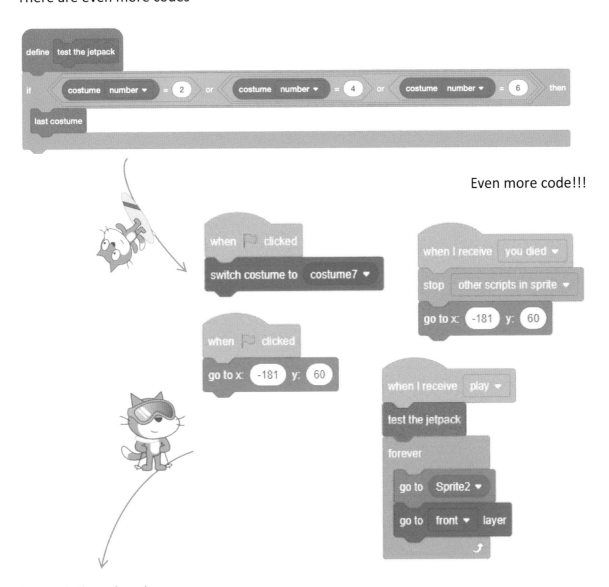

Even more code!!!

Step6: let's make a button

Step7: Enter the code for the button. Get the mp3 music from YouTube and download it.

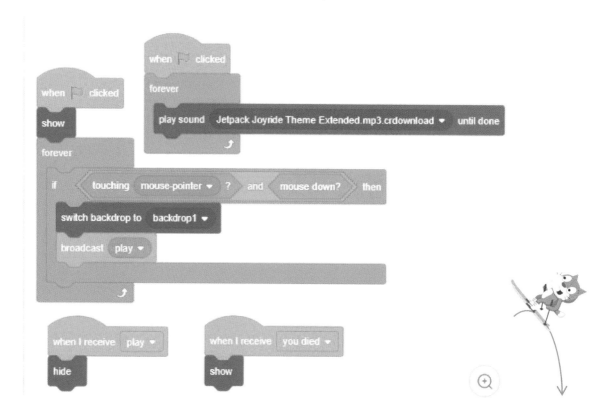

Step8: make a new sprite and name it coin

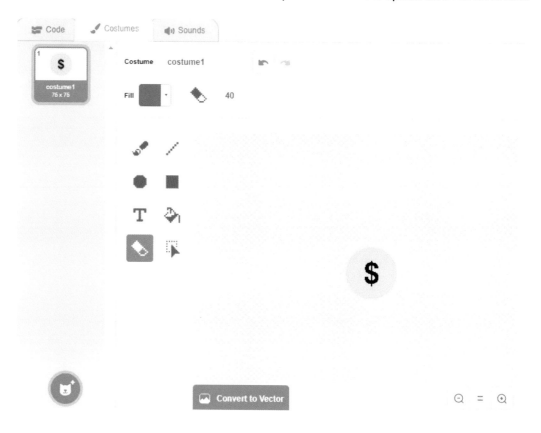

Step9: Enter the code for the coin

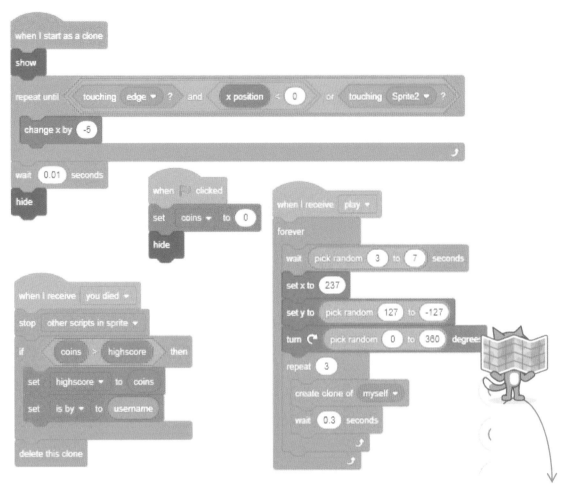

Step10: make a new sprite and name its electric shock

Step11: Enter the code for the electric shock

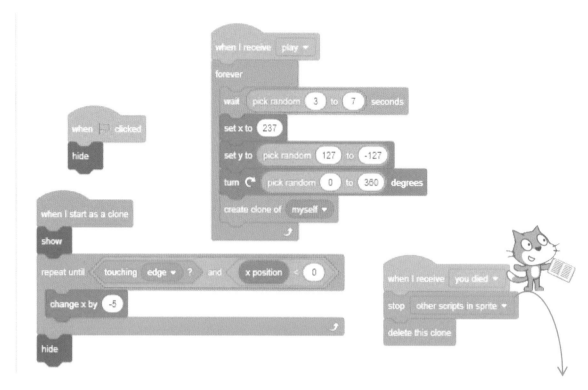

Step12: make 2 new backdrops, backdrop1 and backdrop2

Step13: Enter the code for the backdrop

Now you have finished making the Jet Pack Joy Ride project.

Special thanks to Halfbrick Studios for this game

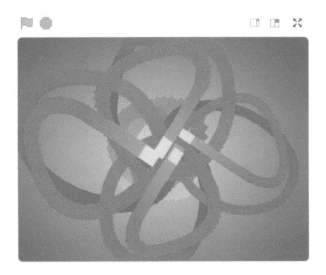

PROJECT INTRODUCTION/RULES

In this project there will be six rectangles, which will move in the opossite direction to your mouse pointer and create a swirl pattern as they go

Sprite	Backdrops
6x	

Step1: Delete the cat

Step2: Make a new sprite and put in a rectangle

Step3: Duplicate the rectangle five times.

Now you should have six rectangles

Step4: Enter the code for the first rectangle

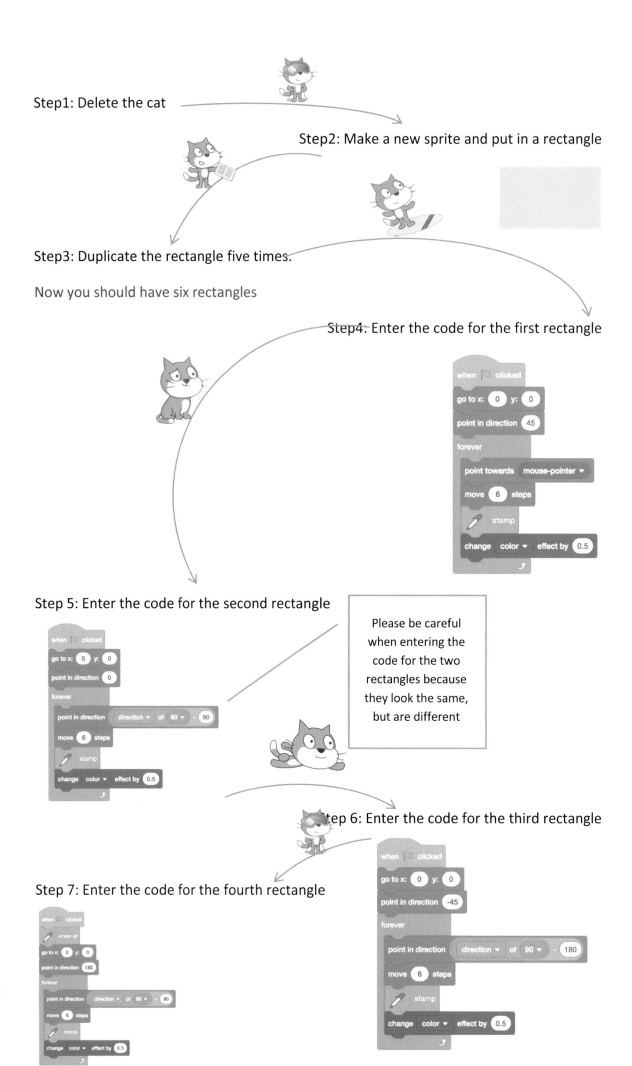

```
when clicked
go to x: 0 y: 0
point in direction 45
forever
    point towards mouse-pointer
    move 6 steps
    stamp
    change color effect by 0.5
```

Step 5: Enter the code for the second rectangle

```
when clicked
go to x: 0 y: 0
point in direction 0
forever
    point in direction direction of 90 - 90
    move 6 steps
    stamp
    change color effect by 0.5
```

Please be careful when entering the code for the two rectangles because they look the same, but are different

Step 6: Enter the code for the third rectangle

```
when clicked
go to x: 0 y: 0
point in direction -45
forever
    point in direction direction of 90 - 180
    move 6 steps
    stamp
    change color effect by 0.5
```

Step 7: Enter the code for the fourth rectangle

```
when clicked
    erase all
go to x: 0 y: 0
point in direction 180
forever
    point in direction direction of 90 + 90
    move 6 steps
    stamp
    change color effect by 0.5
```

Step 8: Enter the code for the fifth rectangle

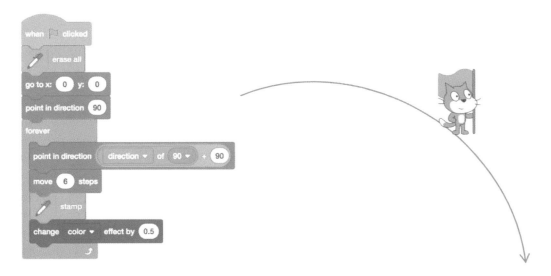

Step 9: Enter the code for the sixth rectangle

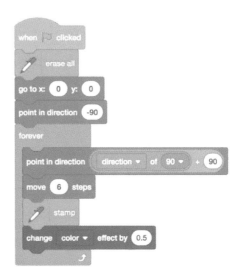

Now you have finished making the Swirl Maker project

PROJECT INTRODUCTION/RULES

If you play Minecraft, you might know these characters. Minecraft is very famous among players, but have you ever seen Minecraft sprites dancing? This project shows how to make the Minecraft sprites dance.

If you click the number 1 key then the zombie will pop up

If you click number 2 key the pig will pop up

If you click number 3 key all the Minecraft sprites pop up

Sprites	Backdrop
	Paint the backdrop black

Step1: delete the cat and go to a new scratch tab

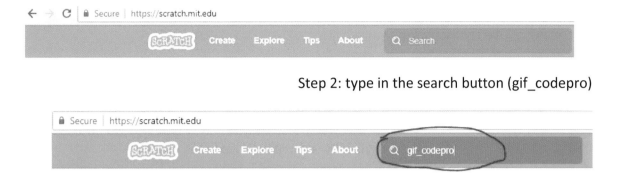

Step 2: type in the search button (gif_codepro)

Step 3: there would be a Minecraft project. Click on that.

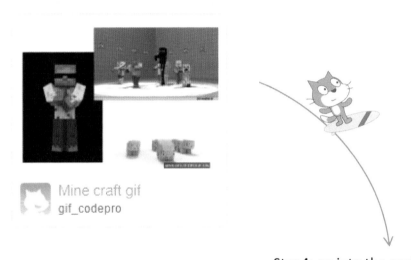

Step4: go into the project by clicking see inside

Step5: export and save all of the three sprites to files on your local computer.

Step6: after you have exported the sprites to your local computer click on the backdrop, and go to Sounds, right click on the Michael Jackson song, Export and save it on your local computer.

Step7: Go back to your project and click on the Upload sprite button

Step8: click on the sprites you downloaded above.

Do this three times with the other sprites

Step9: go to the backdrop, select the Sounds tab, and import the song by selecting Choose a Sound, then Upload Sound

Step10: Enter the code for the zombie sprite (picgifs-minecraft-1105739)

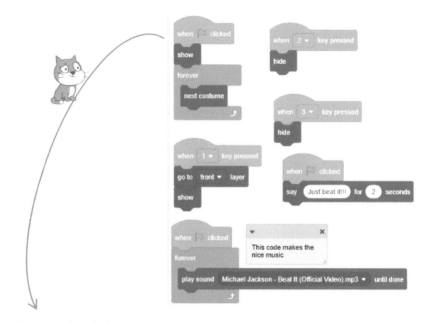

Step11: Enter the code for the pigs (giphy)

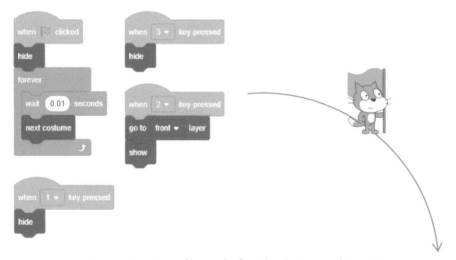

Step12: Enter the code for the last one (tumblr_mx4auvpgYu1t4joh0o1_500)

Step13: Paint the backdrop black

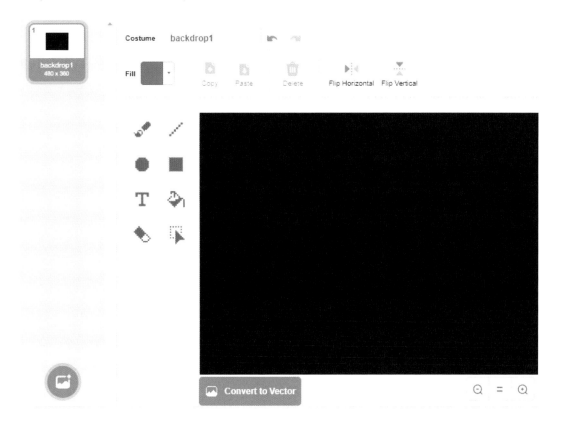

If you want, you can change the backdrop to what every you like

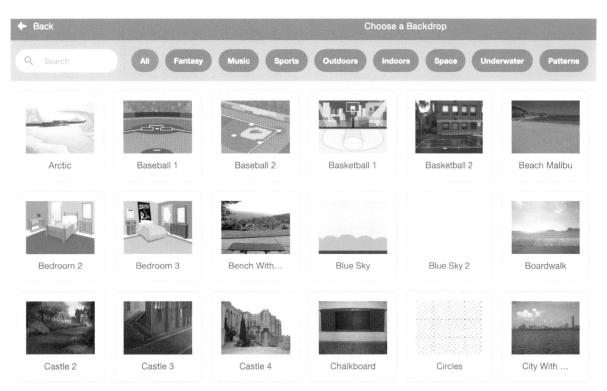

Now you have finished making the Minecraft Studio Dancing project.

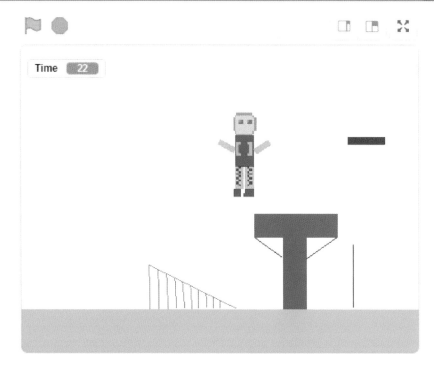

PROJECT INTRODUCTION/RULES

If you play Parkour on your device, it might be easy, but if you do it in real life it would be difficult. You are the mini stick man who has to reach to the end of the level, while performing parkour. To control the stick man, you use the arrow keys to move him and the up arrow or space key to make him jump.

Sprite	Backdrop
	You win !!!

Step1: delete the cat and make a new stick man sprite

Try to make the sprite colourful and creative

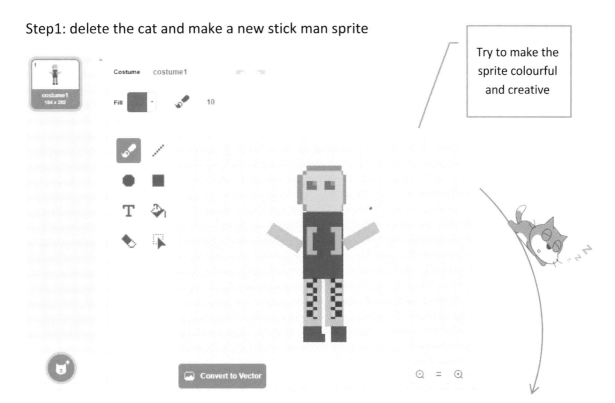

Step2: Enter the code for the stick man.

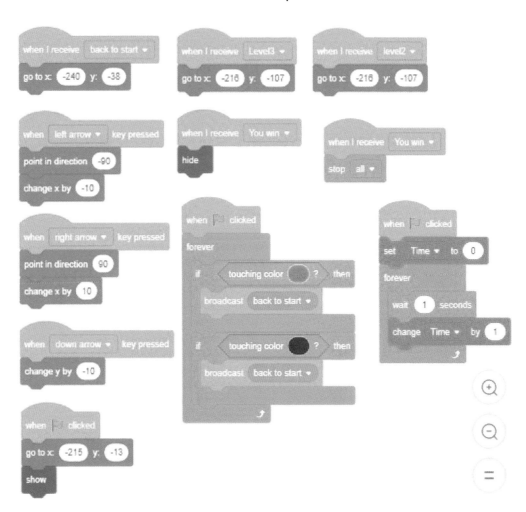

Even more code! This code this is very large so I split it in half, after you have built both pieces, connect them together to make one big code block.

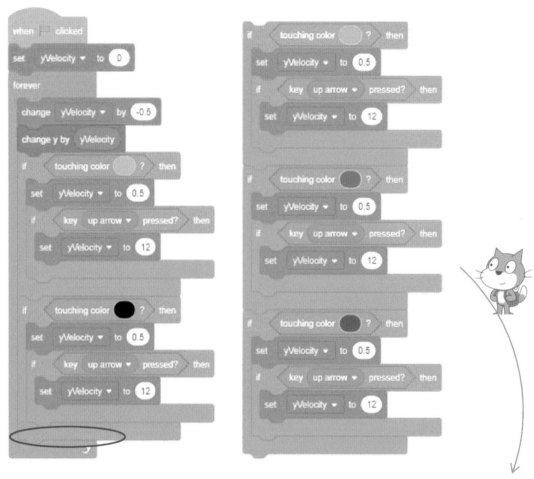

Now connect them together where the red lines are on the diagrams.

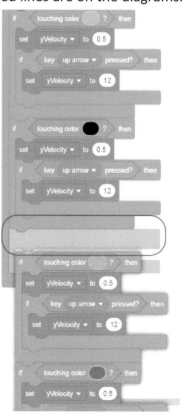

Step3: make a new sprite and draw a long line from top to bottom. **Remember to turn it into bitmap**

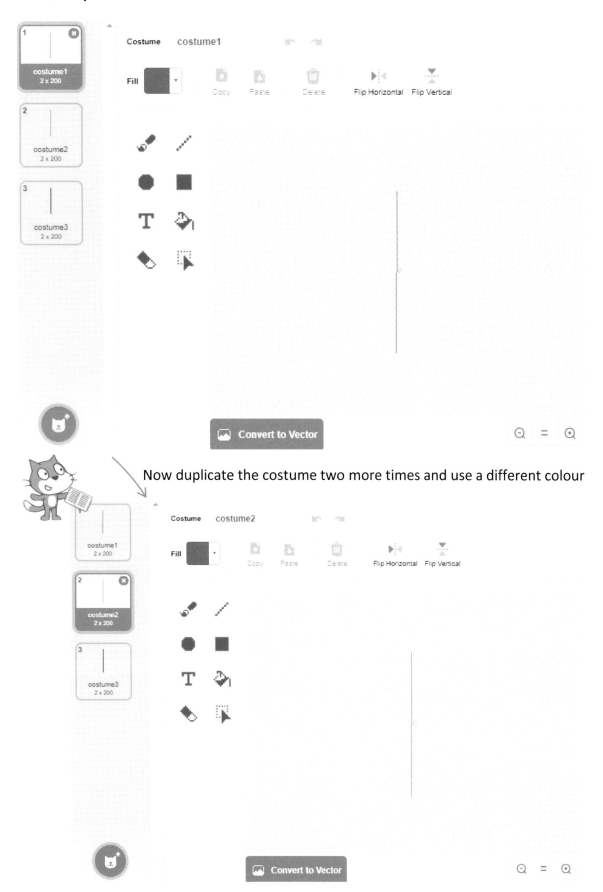

Now duplicate the costume two more times and use a different colour

And also make a costume with a pink colour

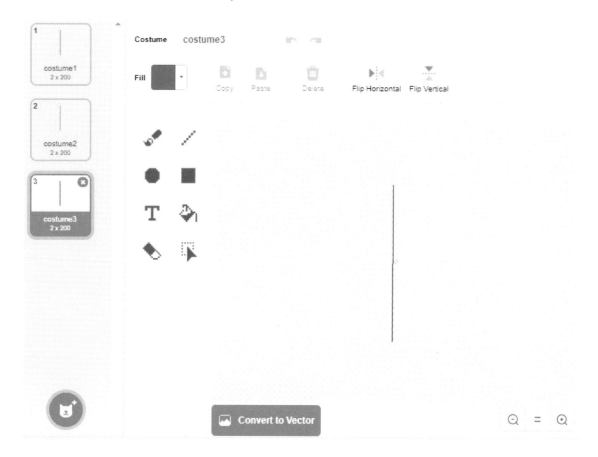

Step4: Enter the code for the line sprite.

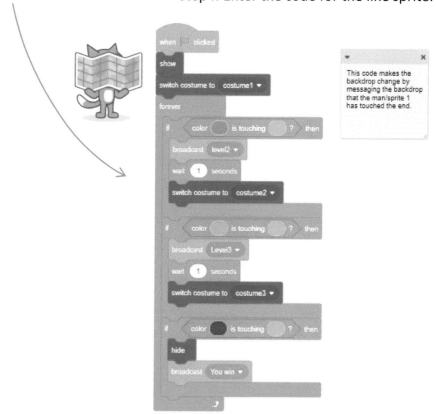

```
when clicked
show
switch costume to costume1
forever
    if color ( ) is touching ( ) ? then
        broadcast level2
        wait 1 seconds
        switch costume to costume2
        if color ( ) is touching ( ) ? then
            broadcast Level3
            wait 1 seconds
            switch costume to costume3
            if color ( ) is touching ( ) ? then
                hide
                broadcast You win
```

This code makes the backdrop change by messaging the backdrop that the man/sprite 1 has touched the end.

Step5: Make three new backdrops and make them have obstacles. You can make them the same as these below, but if you want to you can change them.

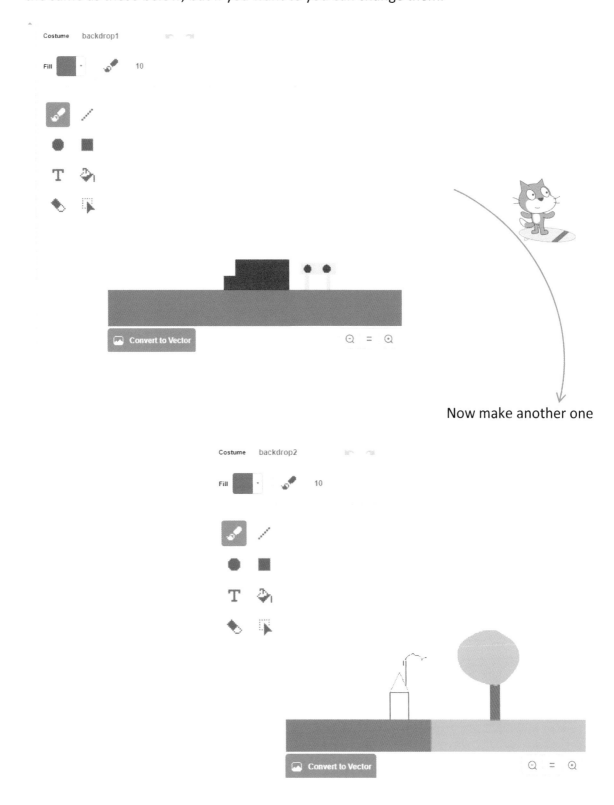

Now make another one

Now make a third one

Step5: when you finish the level you always must have an ending. Let's make a new backdrop which says "You win!!!"

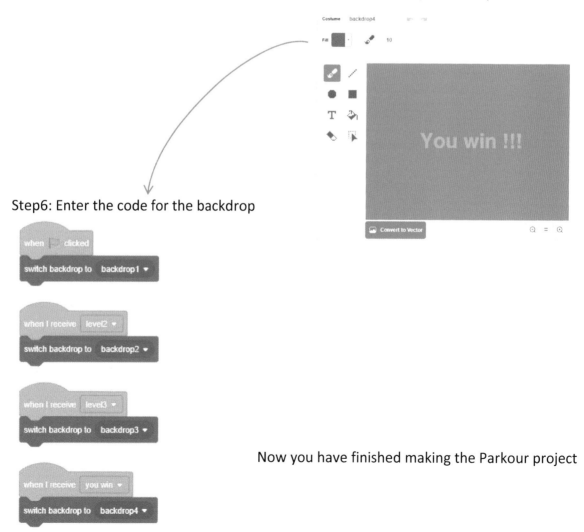

Step6: Enter the code for the backdrop

Now you have finished making the Parkour project

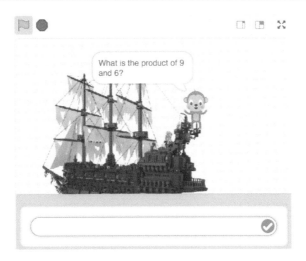

PROJECT INTRODUCTION/RULES

Have your teachers ever asked you to doa maths quiz? Well now you can write a maths quiz in code. As well as doing maths, you can also learn coding.

Sprite	Backdrops
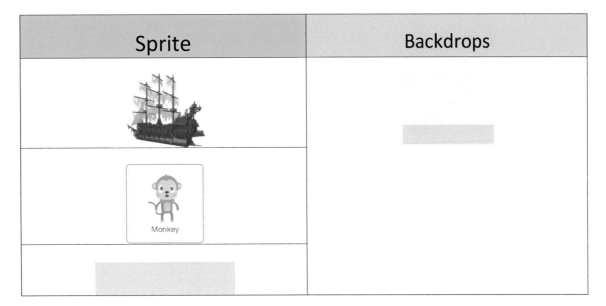	

Step1: Delete the cat

Step2: go to a new tab and type 'scratch'

Step3: In the search bar in scratch type in "gif_codepro

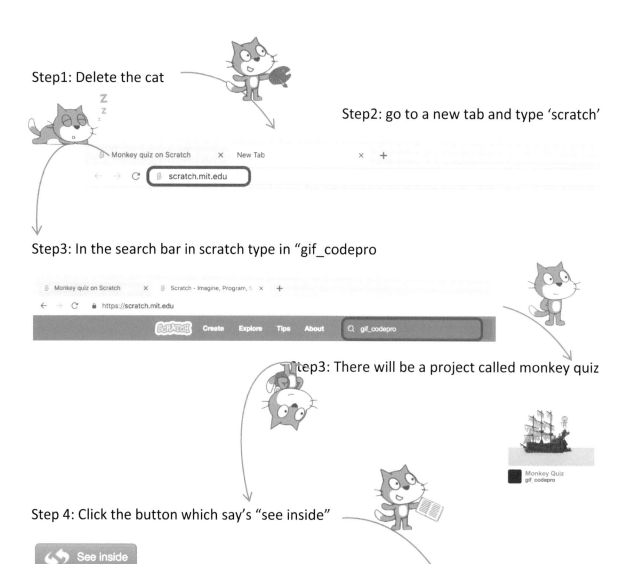

Step3: There will be a project called monkey quiz

Monkey Quiz
gif_codepro

Step 4: Click the button which say's "see inside"

See inside

Step 5: SaveDownload all the sprites to your computer, and then upload them into your own project.

Step 6: Enter the code for the monkey

Since the code is quite large, we have broken it into 3 parts

```
ask join username buys a pen for $1.80, and it pays with $5. How much change does it get? and wait
if   answer = 3.20  then
  say Excellent! for 2 seconds
else
  say Oh noo!!! for 2 seconds
  say ahh for 2 seconds
  move 10 steps
  turn ↻ 90 degrees
  glide 5 secs to x: 146 y: -120
  stop all ▾

ask What's 123+50 and wait
if   answer = 173  then
  say You're doing well! for 2 seconds
else
  say Oh noo!!! for 2 seconds
  say ahh for 2 seconds
  move 10 steps
  turn ↻ 90 degrees
  glide 5 secs to x: 146 y: -120
  stop all ▾

ask What's 121 divided by 11? and wait
if   answer = 11  then
  say Yay! It's correct! for 2 seconds
else
  say Oh noo!!! for 2 seconds
  say ahh for 2 seconds
  move 10 steps
  turn ↻ 90 degrees
  glide 5 secs to x: 146 y: -120
  stop all ▾

ask What's the area of a square if the length is 5cm? and wait

if   answer = 25  then
  say Fabulous! for 2 seconds
else
  say Oh noo!!! for 2 seconds
  say ahh for 2 seconds
  move 10 steps
  turn ↻ 90 degrees
  glide 5 secs to x: 146 y: -120
  stop all ▾

ask What's is 20 times 3? and wait
if   answer = 60  then
  say Good work! for 2 seconds
else
  say Oh noo!!! for 2 seconds
  say ahh for 2 seconds
  move 10 steps
  turn ↻ 90 degrees
  glide 5 secs to x: 146 y: -120
  stop all ▾

say That is the end, and I hope you enjoyed it! Please love and favourite!Also, please follow me!!!! for 4 seconds
```

Now connect them together.

Step 7: Enter the code for the water

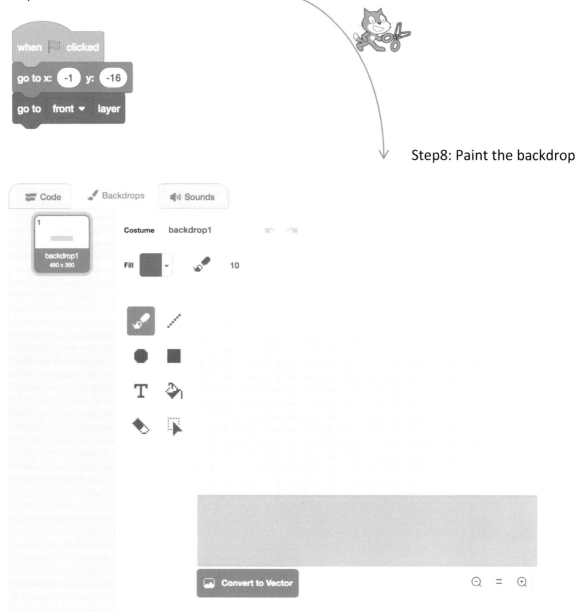

Step8: Paint the backdrop

Now you have finished making the Monkey Quiz project.

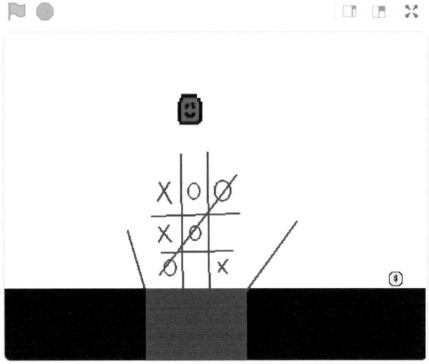

PROJECT INTRODUCTION/RULES

There are many platformer games, but there are comparatively few pixellated platformer games. By adding a pixellated image to your character, you can make the game more creative. To control the mini head you use the arrow keys and you press space bar to jump. Don't touch the red lava or you will have to start again.

Sprite	Backdrop
(mini head pixel sprite)	(black platform)
($ coin)	(platform with tic-tac-toe)
YOU WON!	(L-shaped platform)
	(gray block)

Step1: Delete the cat, and make a new sprite called Mario

To see individual pixels you have to enlarge the image by clicking the magnifying glass icon.

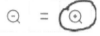

Step2: Enter the code for the sprite

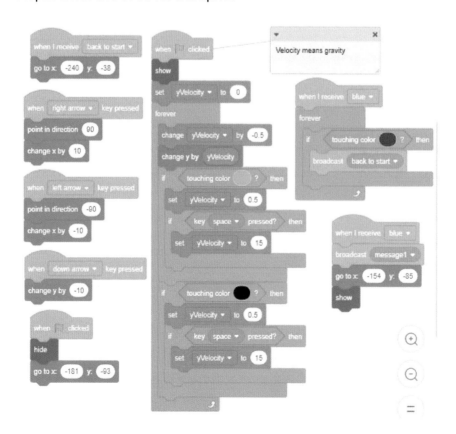

Step3: create a new sprite and name it coin

Step4: Enter the code for the coin

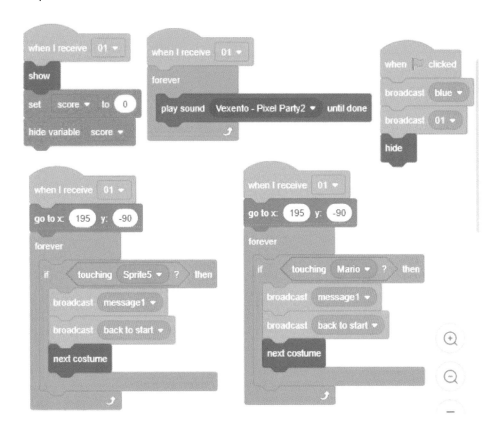

Even more codes!!!

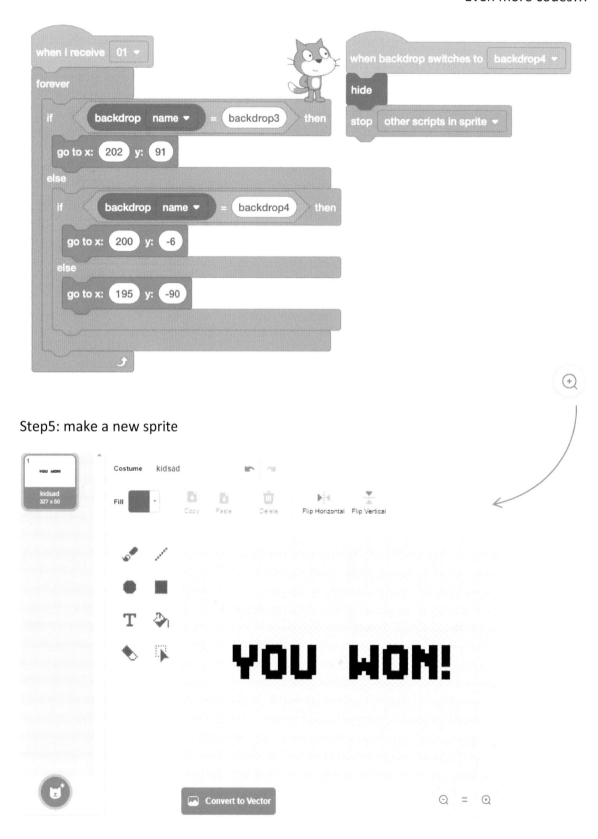

when I receive 01 ▼
forever
  if ⟨ backdrop name ▼ = backdrop3 ⟩ then
    go to x: 202 y: 91
  else
    if ⟨ backdrop name ▼ = backdrop4 ⟩ then
      go to x: 200 y: -6
    else
      go to x: 195 y: -90

when backdrop switches to backdrop4 ▼
  hide
  stop other scripts in sprite ▼

Step5: make a new sprite

Costume   kidsad

Fill

Copy   Paste   Delete   Flip Horizontal   Flip Vertical

T

YOU WON!

Convert to Vector

Step6: Enter the code for this sprite

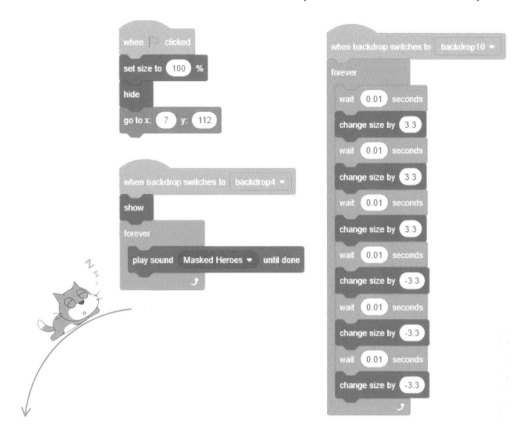

Step7: make 4 new backdrops and you have to make it into a platformer like these.

Backdrop 1

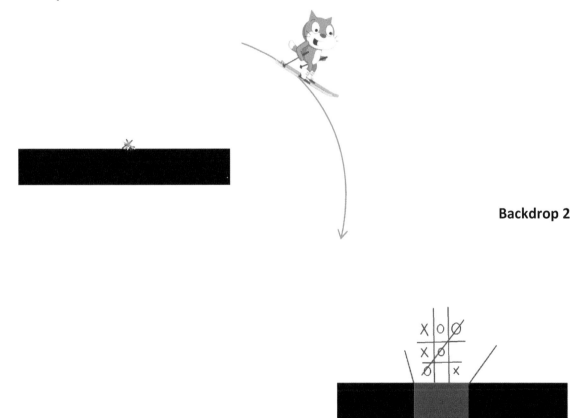

Backdrop 2

Backdrop 3

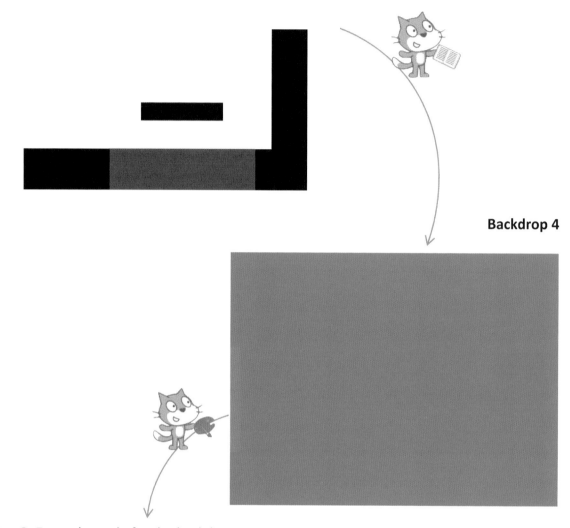

Backdrop 4

Step8: Enter the code for the backdrop

Now you have finished making the High Jump Platformer project.

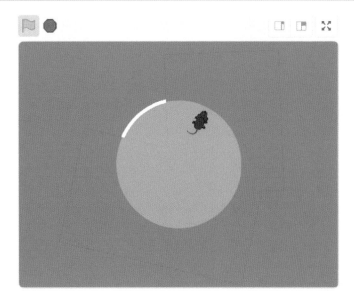

PROJECT INTRODUCTION/RULES

In this game you have to use your mouse pointer to control the white curve line to block the mouse from escaping the circle. The mouse is trapped and you have to keep it trapped. If the mouse goes out of the circle, the game will stop. Thanks to @Google_Network for this project

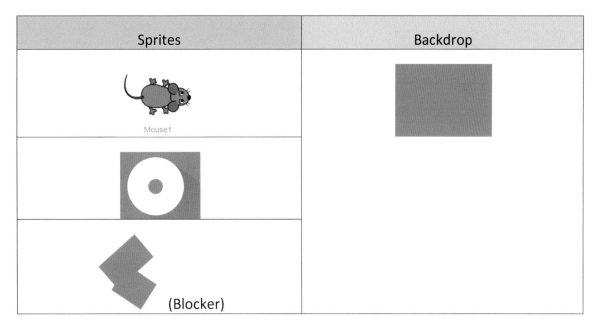

Sprites	Backdrop
Mouse1	
(Blocker)	

Step 1: delete the cat and get a mouse sprite

Mouse1

Step2: Enter the code for the mouse. **Before you start making this code get all the sprites**

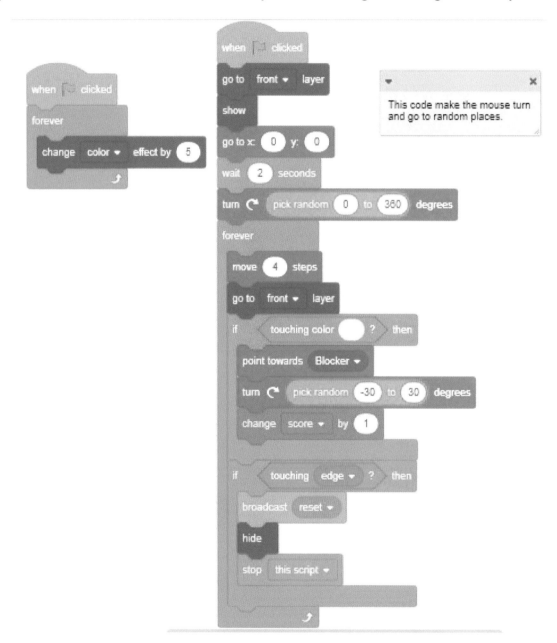

when 🏳 clicked
go to front layer
show
go to x: 0 y: 0
wait 2 seconds
turn ↻ pick random 0 to 360 degrees
forever
  move 4 steps
  go to front layer
  if touching color ? then
  point towards Blocker
  turn ↻ pick random -30 to 30 degrees
  change score by 1
  if touching edge ? then
  broadcast reset
  hide
  stop this script

when 🏳 clicked
forever
  change color effect by 5

This code make the mouse turn and go to random places.

Step3: make a new sprite. Draw it to look the same as the picture below.

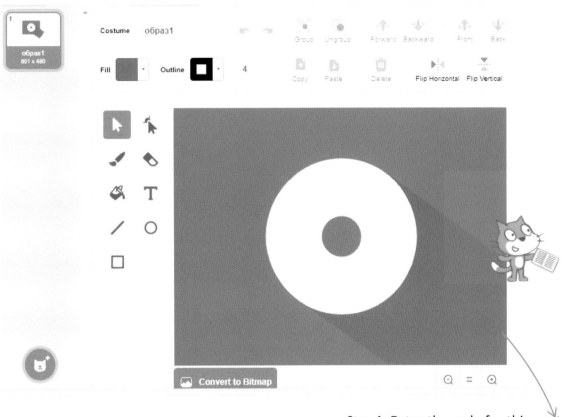

Step4: Enter the code for this sprite

Step5: make a new sprite and draw the same as the picture below

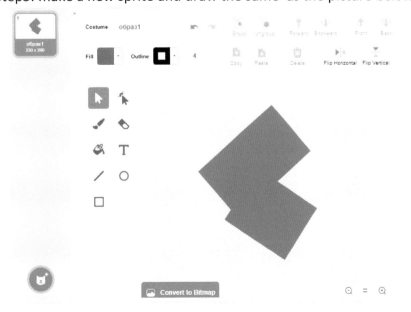

Step 6: Enter the code for this sprite

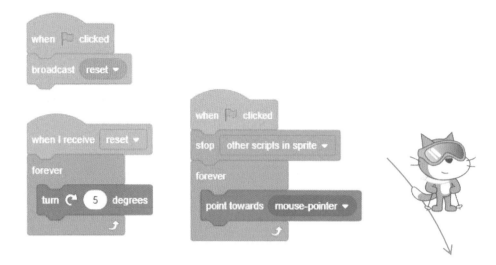

Step7: make a new sprite and draw it the same as the picture below

Step8: Enter the code for this sprite

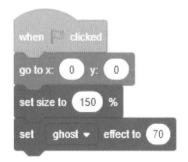

Step9: Create a backdrop. Paint it the same colour as you did with the sprites you drew.

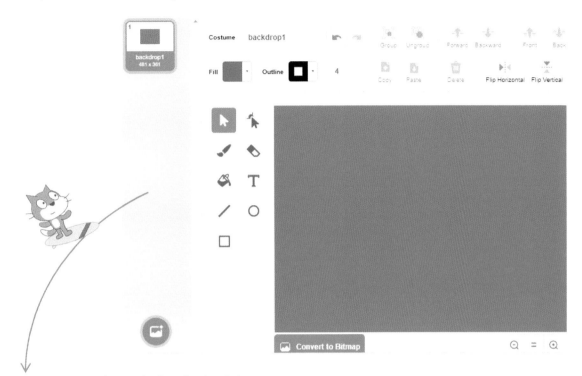

Step 10: Enter the code for the backdrop

Now you have finished making the Circle Mouse project.

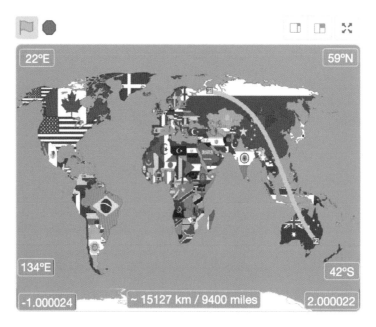

PROJECT INTRODUCTION/RULES

In this project you have to drag the two sprites, p1 and p2, from one country to another to see the distance between the two countries. This project is mainly about mathematics. This project is long so remember to test and check your codes.

Sprites	Backdrop
Sprite1	
P1 Sprite2	
P2 Sprite3	

Step 1: Delete the cat. Make a new sprite (Choose a Sprite / Paint) but don't draw anything in it just yet.

Step2: Enter the code for the new sprite

IMPORTANT – you will not be able to enter some of this code until you have created the other sprites

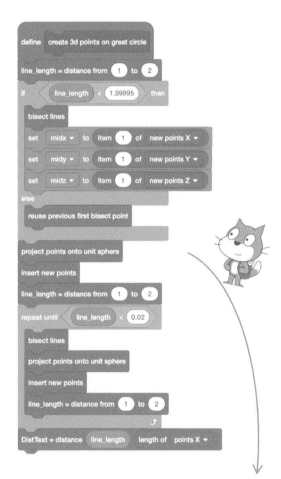

Even more!!!!

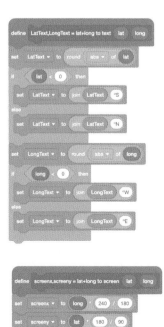

Even more code!!!

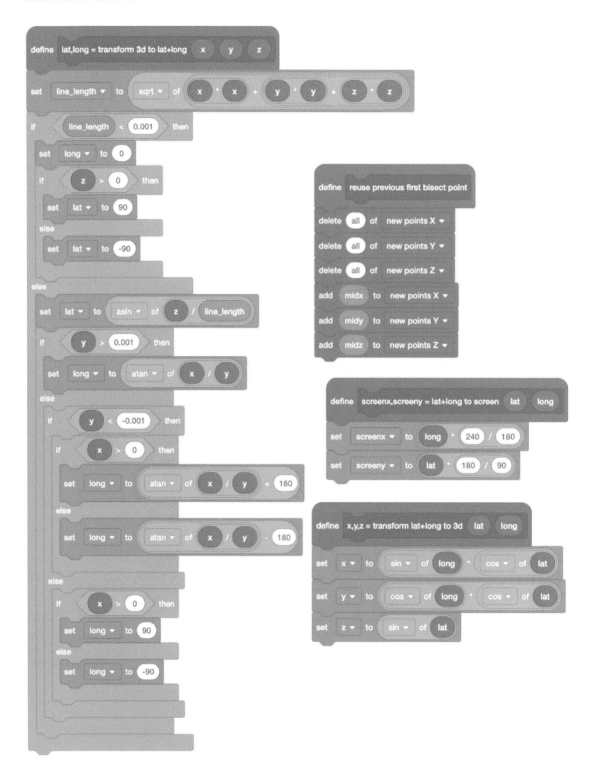

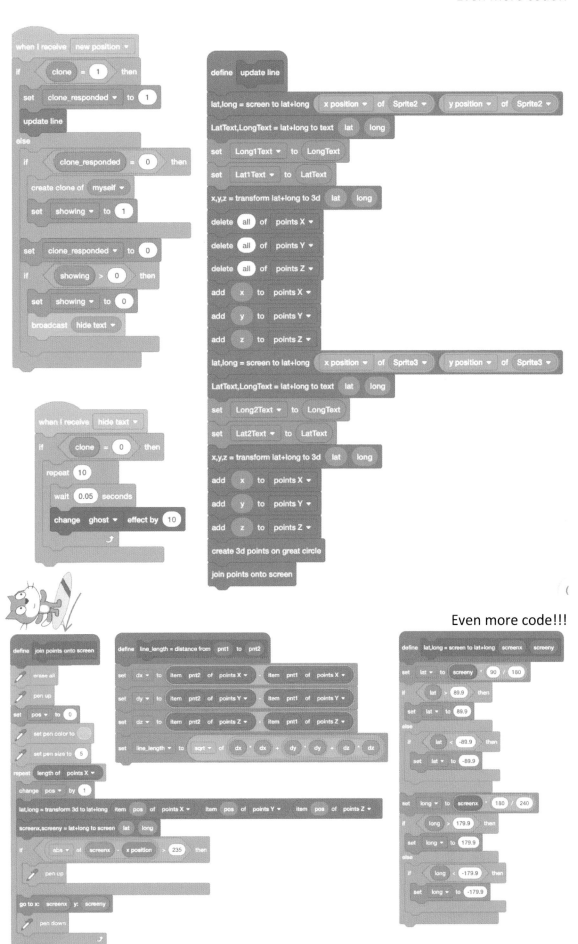

Even more codes!!!

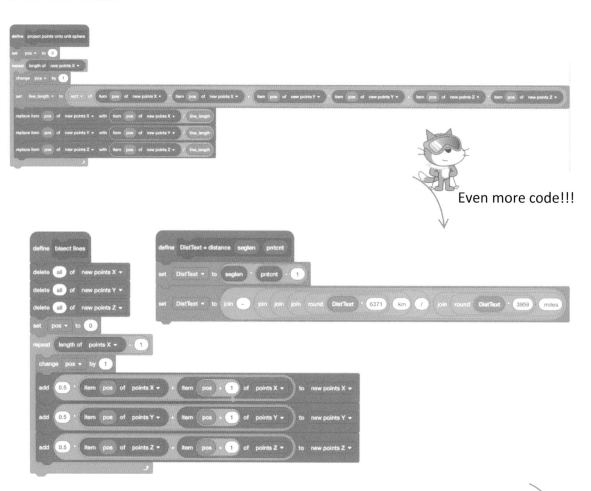

Even more code!!!

Step 3: Create and paint the P1 sprite. It must be named Sprite2. Enter the code for Sprite2

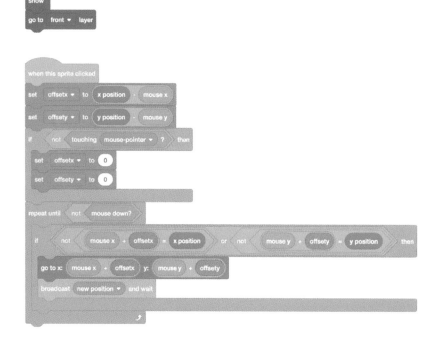

Step 4: Create and paint the P2 Sprite. It must be named Sprite3. Enter the code for Sprite3

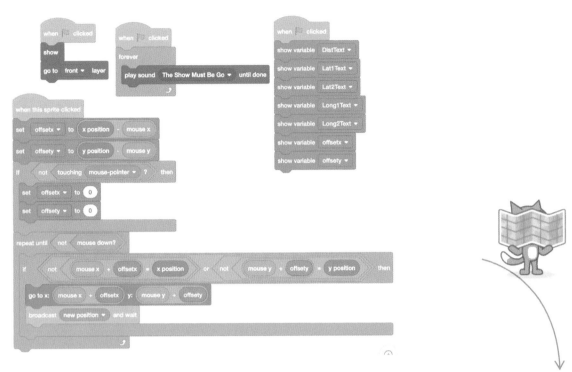

Step 5: Go to Google and find a map which looks like this. Put this into your backdrop

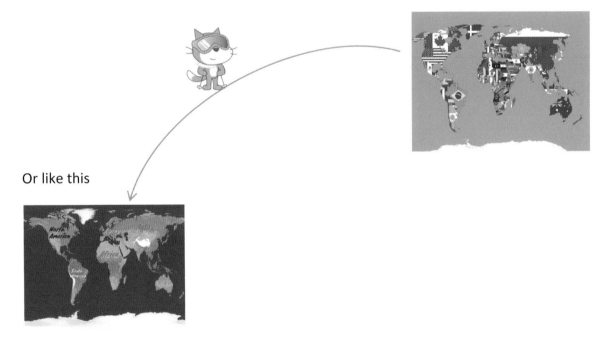

Or like this

Copy the map into

Now you have finished with this project.

Thanks to DadOfMrLog for the Project

On the 1st of February 2019 this project was featured by the Scratch team!!!!

PROJECT INTRODUCTION/RULES

This is another platformer game where you use your arrow keys to move, and the space bar to jump. You can land on the orange, but if you touch the red then you have to start again.

Sprites	Backdrop

Step1: Delete the cat and get a dinosaur sprite from the library

Step 2: Get these two backdrops from the library and draw the coloured rectangles and circle onto the Jurassic backdrop.

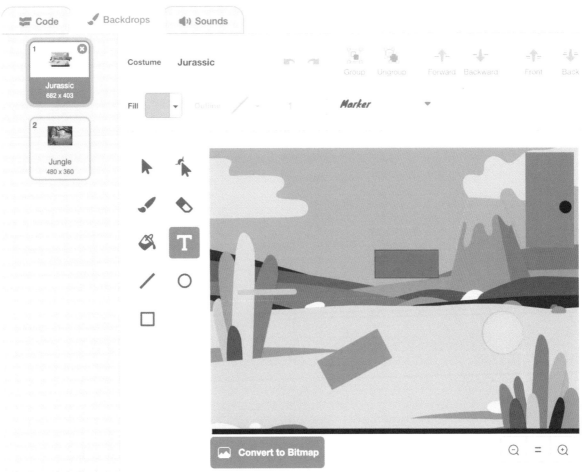

And the second backdrop, Jungle. Click Convert to Bitmap, and then draw "You Win!!" over the top using the Text tool. Use the Marker font if you want your text to look like mine.

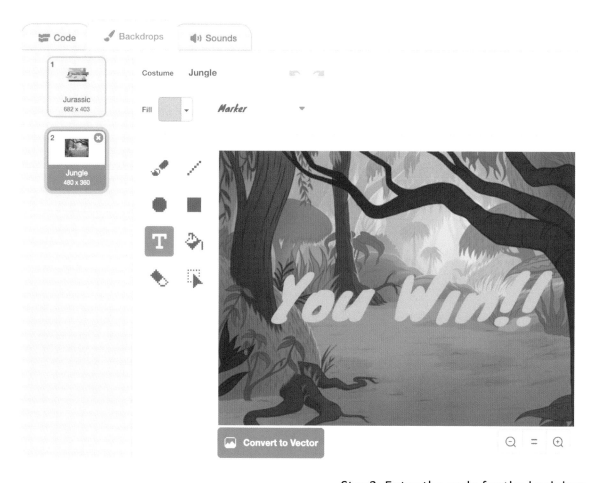

Step3: Enter the code for the backdrop

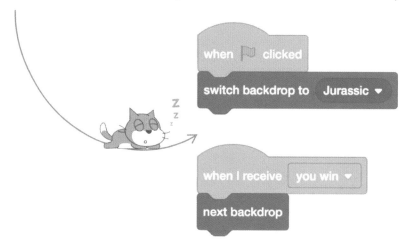

Step 4: Enter the code for the Dinosaur

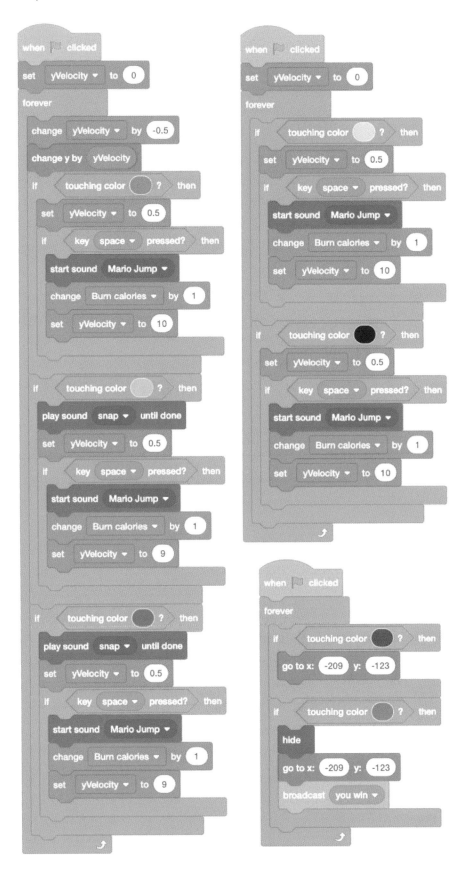

Even more code!!!

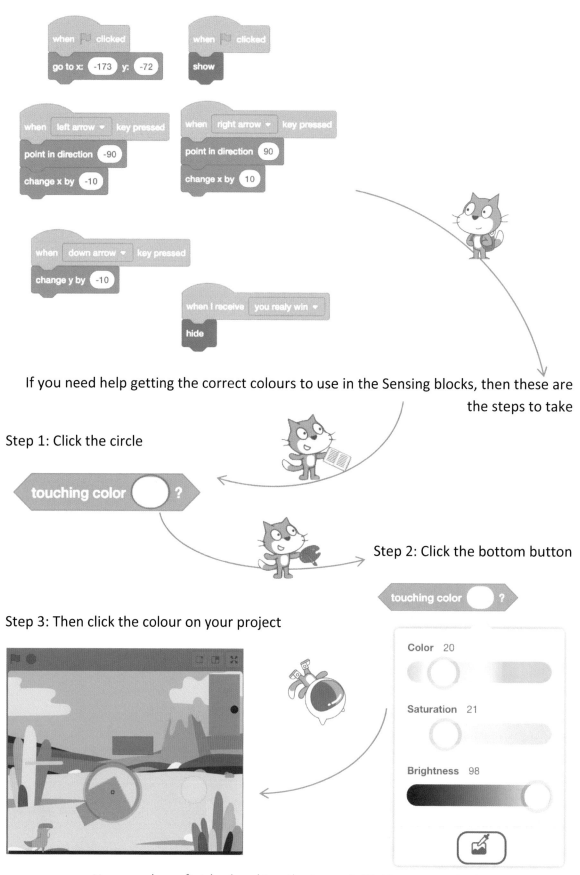

If you need help getting the correct colours to use in the Sensing blocks, then these are the steps to take

Step 1: Click the circle

Step 2: Click the bottom button

Step 3: Then click the colour on your project

Now you have finished making the Jurassic Platformer project.

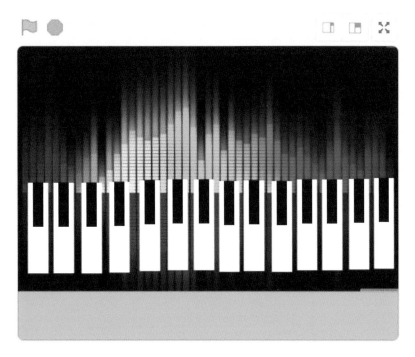

PROJECT INTRODUCTION/RULES

You might have played piano on a keyboard, but have you ever played a digital piano? This game uses piano notes to make music. You can click any keys between {Q,W,E,R,T,Y,U,I,O,P,A,S,D,F} keys to play music notes. Have fun with this game. 😊

Sprites	Backdrop
14x	

Step1: Delete the cat and draw a new sprite that looks like a piano key.

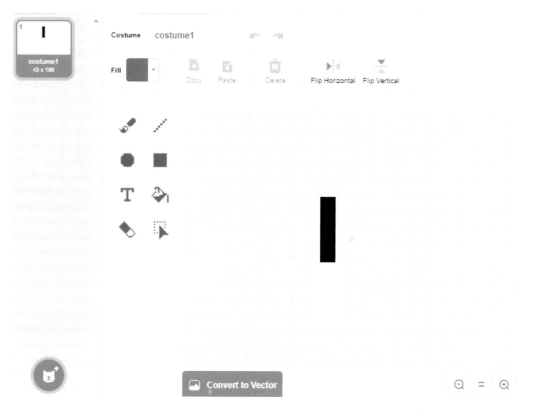

Step2: Enter the code for the sprite

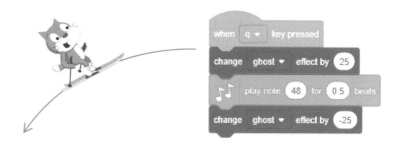

Now duplicate the sprite 13 times, so that you end up with 14 sprites.

Sprite 2 codes

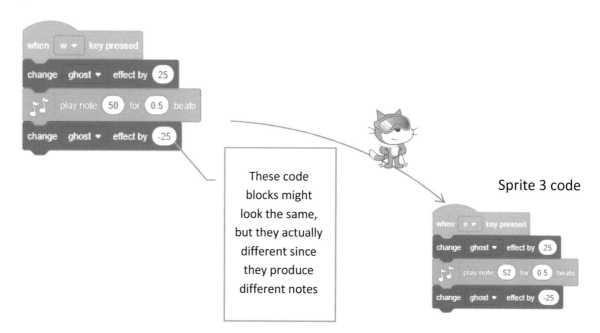

These code blocks might look the same, but they actually different since they produce different notes

Sprite 3 code

Sprite 4 code

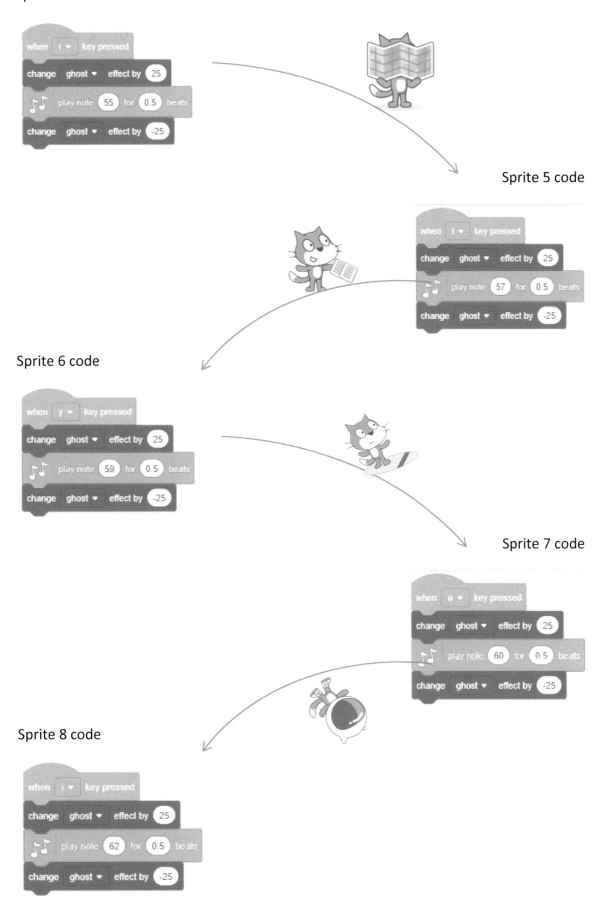

Sprite 5 code

Sprite 6 code

Sprite 7 code

Sprite 8 code

Sprite 9 code

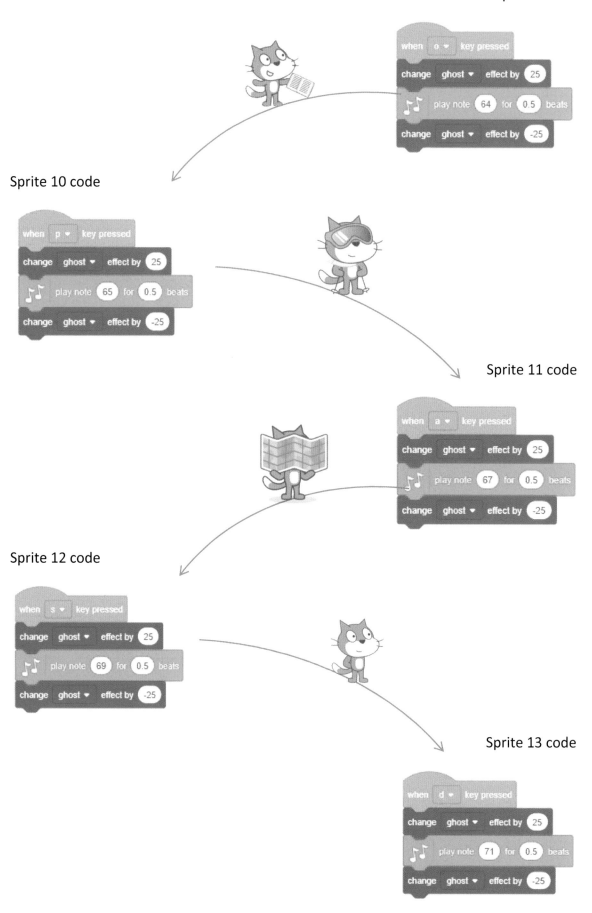

Sprite 10 code

Sprite 11 code

Sprite 12 code

Sprite 13 code

84

Sprite 14 code

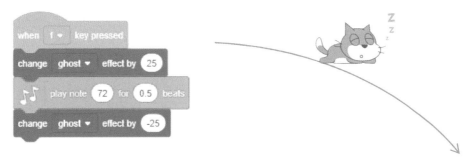

Now you need to include a backdrop. Get a new backdrop by searching the web for music wallpaper. When you found a nice backdrop, save it to your local computer and then upload it into the backdrop of your Scratch project. Remember to arrange the sprites in order

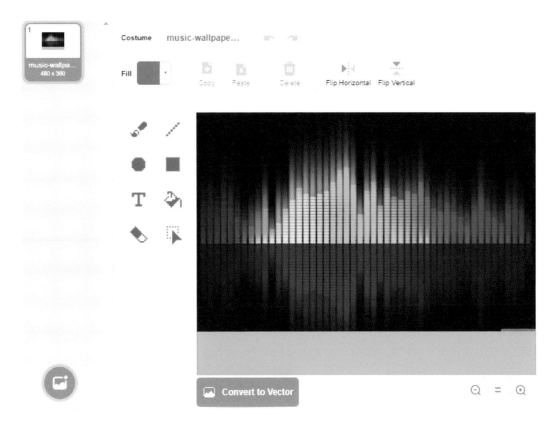

Now you have finished making the Piano project.

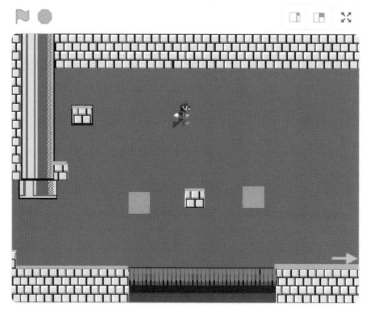

PROJECT INTRODUCTION/RULES

This game is a platformer, but it has a Mario sprite and a Mario backdrop. You have to avoid touching the red area on the bottom. To control the Mario sprite, you use the arrow keys to move, and you press the space bar to jump. This game uses gravity also, so that when you jump Mariowill fall with acceleration, like humans and animals do when they jump.

Sprite	Backdrop

Step1: delete the cat and go to Google and get a nice Mario image and then import it into your Scratch project. Get an image which is transparent (PNG).

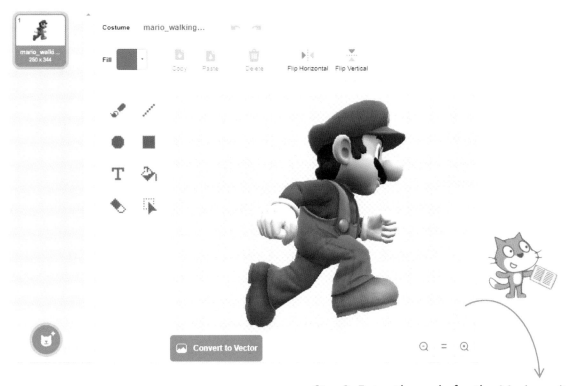

Step2: Enter the code for the Mario sprite

There are even more codes

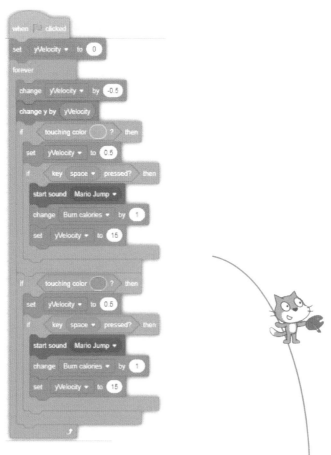

Step3: go to a new tab in your browser and open Scratch. DO NOT DELETE YOUR CURRENT PROJECT.

Step 4: type in the search button (gif_codepro)

Step5: you should see a Mine craft 1 platformer project. Go into that.

Step6: click the See inside button.

Step7: go into to the Backdrop and export the Dungeon2 costume of the backdrop to your local computer....after you have done that, then go back to your project and import the backdrop image into your Scratch project.

Step8: now it should look like this

You have finished the Mario Game 1 project.

PROJECT INTRODUCTION/RULES

This is similar to Mario Game 1, but now we go to level 2. This game is a platformer, but it has a Mario sprite and a Mario backdrop. You have to avoid touching the red areas. To control the Mario you have to use the arrow keys to move and you press the space bar to jump. This game uses gravity also, so that when you jump, you will fall down with acceleration like humans and animals do when they jump.

Sprite	Backdrop

Step1: Delete the cat, and go to Google, get a nice Mario image, and then import it into your Scratch project.

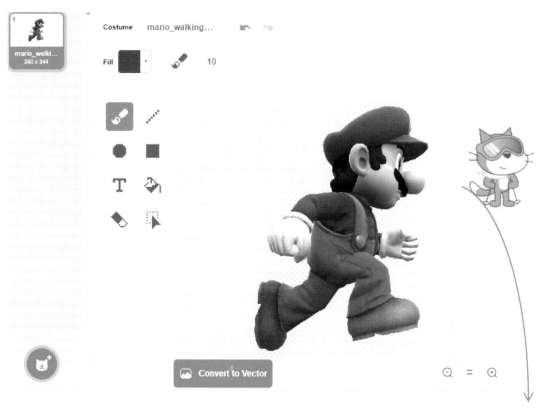

Step2: Enter the code for the Mario sprite

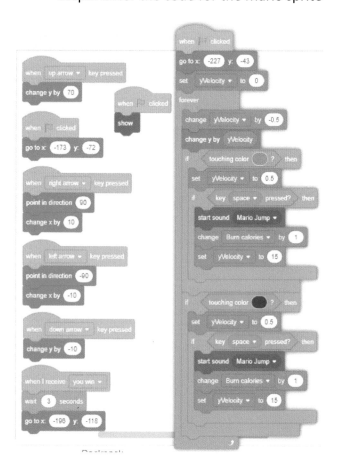

There is even more code

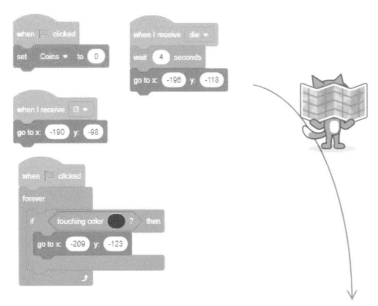

Step3: Go to a new scratch tab. DO NOT DELETE YOUR CURRENT PROJECT

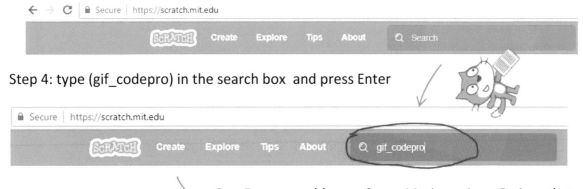

Step 4: type (gif_codepro) in the search box and press Enter

Step5: you would see a Super Mario project. Go into that.

Step6: click the See inside button.

Step7: go to the backdrop and export that backdrop into your local computer, after you have done that then go back to your Scratch project, and click the file button to input it onto your scratch.

Step8: now it should like this

Now you have finished making the Mario Game 2 project

PROJECT INTRODUCTION/RULES

This is a Jurassic World game where you have to shoot and kill the dinosaur from the helicopter. You can only move up and down and you have to press the space bar to shoot.

Sprite	Backdrops
Saver	(forest backdrop)
Bullet 1	You Died!
Bullet 2	
Allosaurus… 2x	

Step1: Delete the cat and go to a new tab and go to scratch and type in "gif_codepro

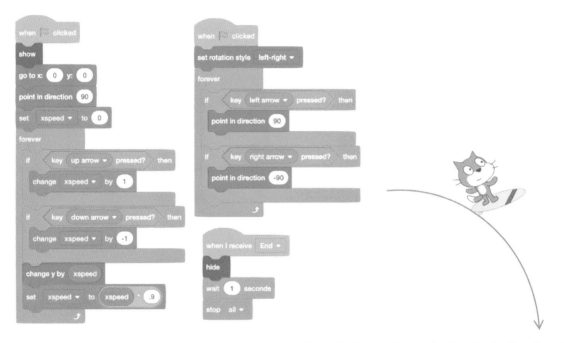

There would be a project called Jurassic world, click that and the click See inside.

Now export all the sprites and the backdrop to your local computer, and then upload them into your current project

Step 2: Enter the code for the helicopter (the sprite called Saver)

Step 3: Enter the code for the Bullet 1 sprite

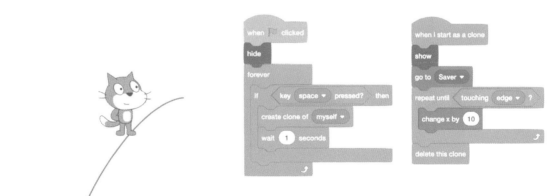

Step 4: Enter the code for the Bullet 2 sprite

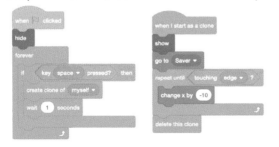

Step 5: Enter the code for the first dinosaur. The sprite is named Allosaurus_europaeus.

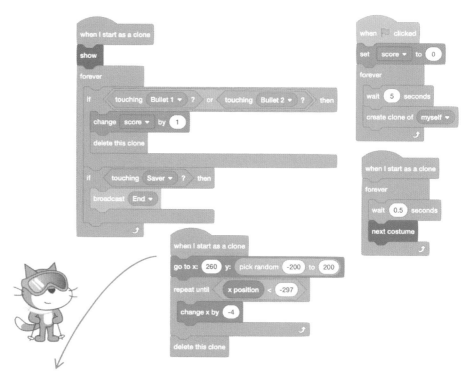

Step 6: Enter the code for the second dinosaur. The sprite is named
Allosaurus_europaeus2

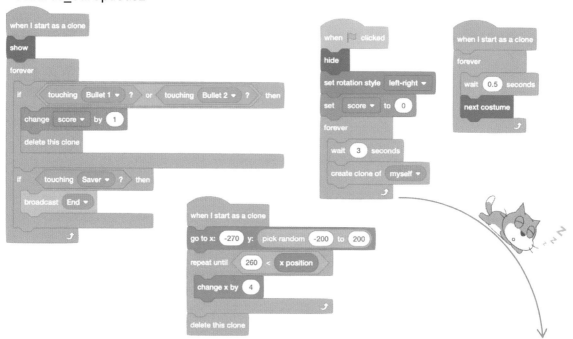

Step 7: Enter the code for the backdrop

Now you have finished making the Jurassic World project

PROJECT INTRODUCTION/RULES

This is an art project where the cat and the beetles make hexagon shapes, using Pen, Control and Motion blocks. You don't have to use any keys for this project.

Sprite	Backdrop
Cat1	Paint the backdrop white
Beetle	

Step 1: get two sprites. I have used the cat and the beetle

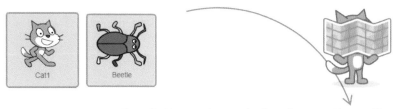

Step2: Enter the code for the cat. You will need a Pen Extention for this

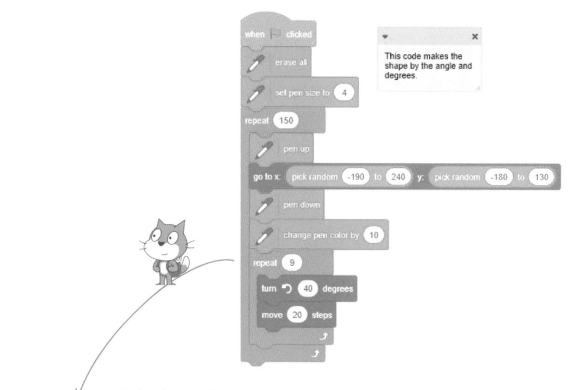

Step3: Enter the code for the beetle

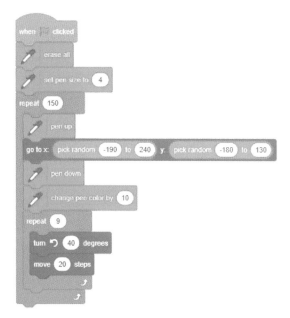

Now you have finished making the Octagon project

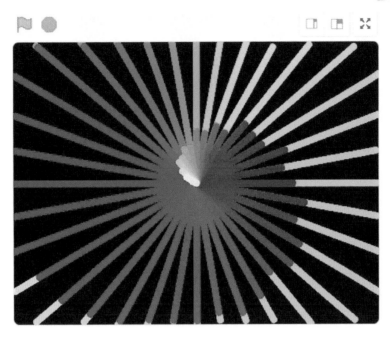

PROJECT INTRODUCTION/RULES

This project is an art project where lines would be spinning making the art above. You don't have to use any keys for this project.

Sprites	Backdrop
Cat1	Paint the backdrop black

Step1: keep the cat and don't delete it.

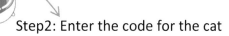

Step2: Enter the code for the cat

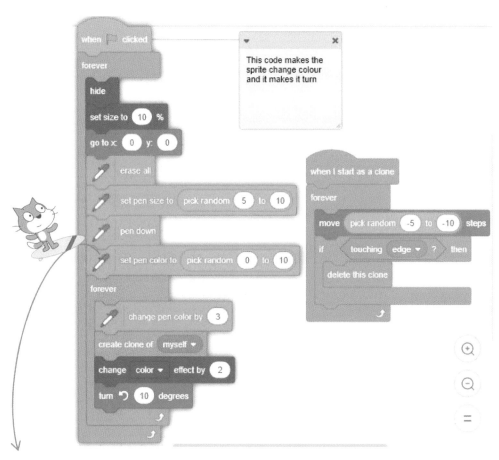

If you want, you can change the backdrop colour

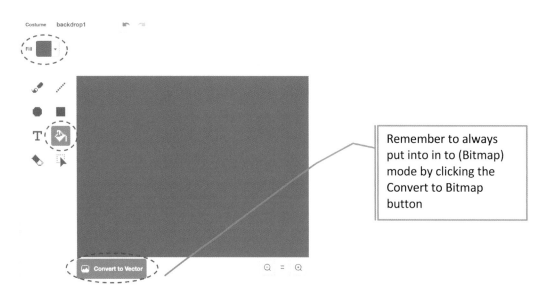

Remember to always put into in to (Bitmap) mode by clicking the Convert to Bitmap button

Now you have finished making the Sting of Art project

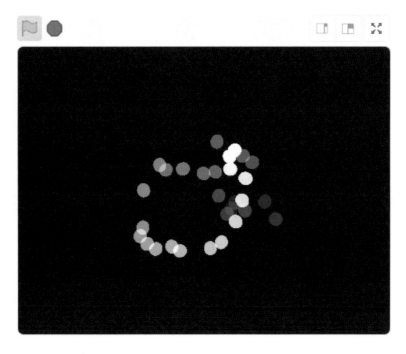

PROJECT INTRODUCTION/RULES

This project is similar tos the Circle Fade project, but this one uses a different colour and it fades more quickly than it did for the other project. You move your mouse pointer around on the screen to produce the art.

Sprites	Backdrop
	Paint the backdrop black

Step1: delete the cat and make a new sprite. Make it a white circle

Step2: Enter the code for this sprite.

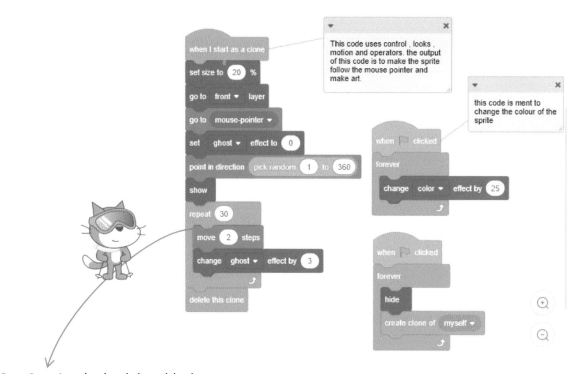

Step3: paint the backdrop black

Now you have finished making this project.

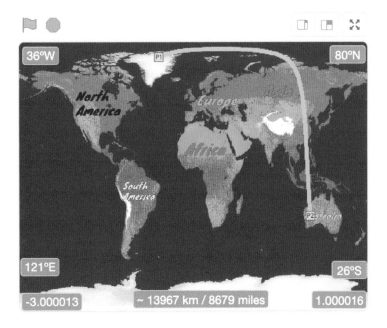

PROJECT INTRODUCTION/RULES

Have you ever wondered how far it is from one place to another? Now you can make a project which will tell you the distance from one place to another. You will be making the same thing as your earlierer Globe Distance project, but you will need to find a backdrop, and you will need to write the names of the continents on the backdrop.

Sprites	Backdrops
P1 Point1	[world map backdrop]
P2 Point2	
Sprite1	

Step1: Delete the cat and make two new sprites

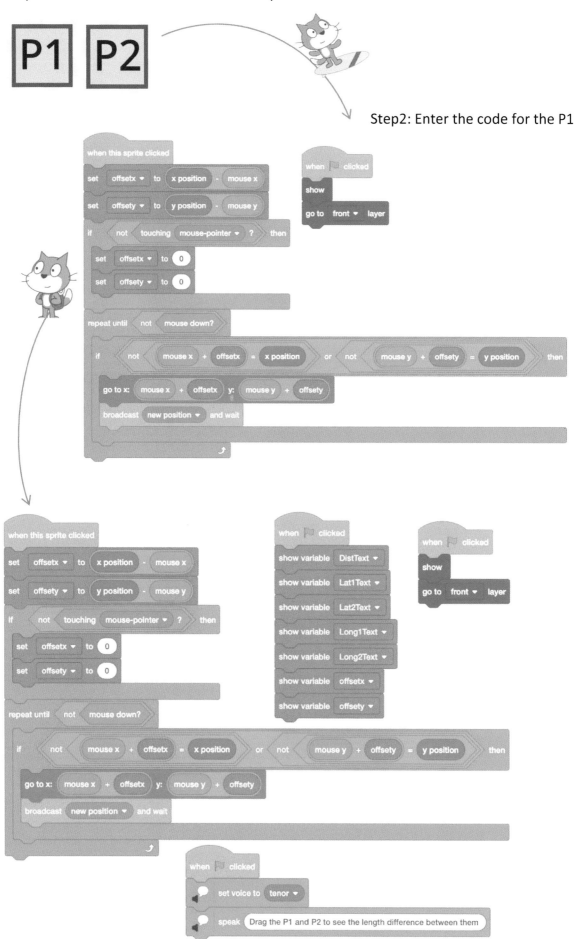

Step2: Enter the code for the P1

Step 4: Make a new sprite but DON'T put anything in it

Sprite1

Step 5: Enter the code for the sprite with nothing in it

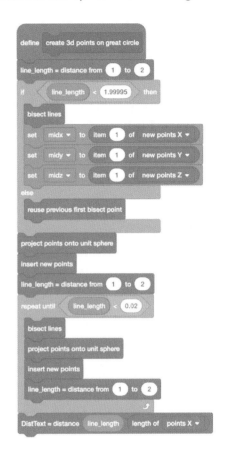

Even more code!!!

Even more code!!!

```
define lat,long = transform 3d to lat+long  x  y  z

set line_length ▼ to ( sqrt ▼ of ( x · x + y · y + z · z ) )

if < line_length < (0.001) > then
    set long ▼ to (0)
    if < z > (0) > then
        set lat ▼ to (90)
    else
        set lat ▼ to (-90)
else
    set lat ▼ to ( asin ▼ of ( z / line_length ) )
    if < y > (0.001) > then
        set long ▼ to ( atan ▼ of ( x / y ) )
    else
        if < y < (-0.001) > then
            if < x > (0) > then
                set long ▼ to ( atan ▼ of ( x / y ) + (180) )
            else
                set long ▼ to ( atan ▼ of ( x / y ) - (180) )
        else
            if < x > (0) > then
                set long ▼ to (90)
            else
                set long ▼ to (-90)
```

Even more code!!!

```
define project points onto unit sphere

set pos ▼ to (0)
repeat ( length of new points X ▼ )
    change pos ▼ by (1)
    set line_length ▼ to ( sqrt ▼ of ( item pos of new points X ▼ · item pos of new points X ▼ + item pos of new points Y ▼ · item pos of new points Y ▼ + item pos of new points Z ▼ · item pos of new points Z ▼ ) )
    replace item pos of new points X ▼ with ( item pos of new points X ▼ / line_length )
    replace item pos of new points Y ▼ with ( item pos of new points Y ▼ / line_length )
    replace item pos of new points Z ▼ with ( item pos of new points Z ▼ / line_length )
```

Even more code!!!

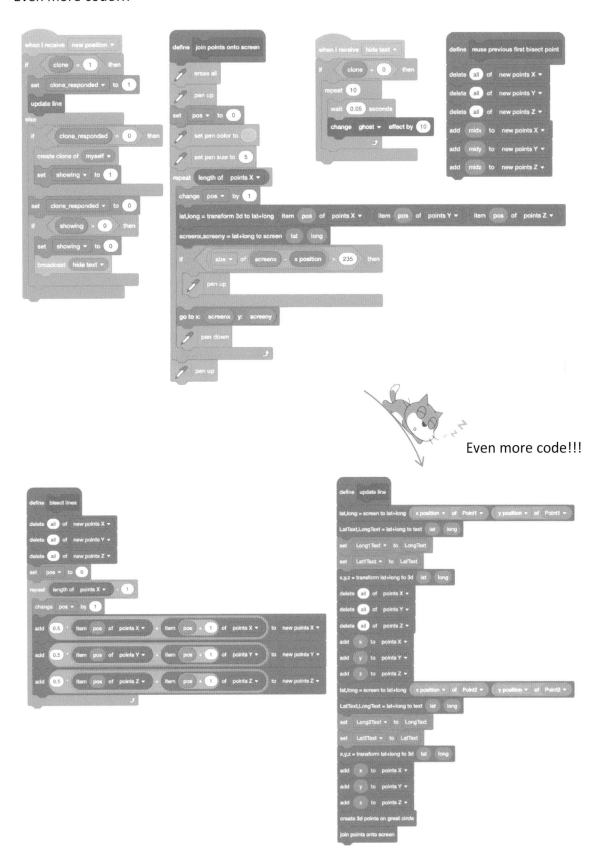

Even more code!!!

Even more code!!!

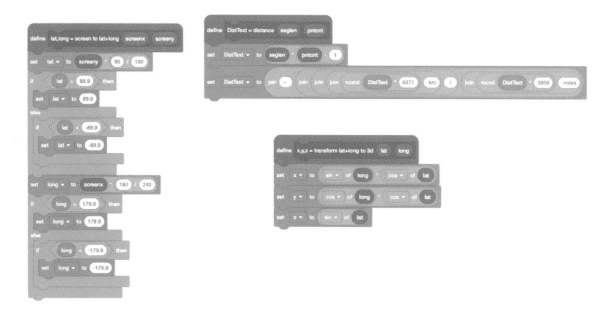

Step 6: Go to a new tab and try to find a map of the world using Google. Once you have found a suitable map, upload it into your project. Try to find a map which looks like mine

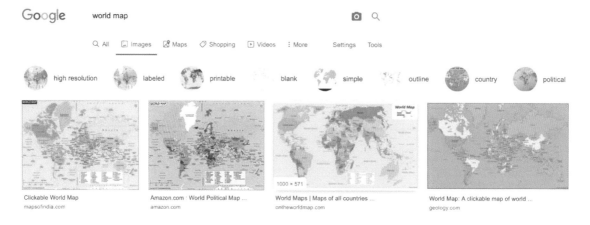

Now you have finished making the Globe Distance 2 project

On the 1 st of February 2019 this project was featured by the Scratch Team!!!

Link to the project→ https://scratch.mit.edu/projects/280537153/

Thanks to DadOfMrLog for the Project

PROJECT INTRODUCTION/RULES

This is the Question Asker, part 2. This is a harder project, since it uses the Operator blocks. Ask your friends or parents to answer the project's questions.

Sprites	Backdrop
Cat1	Paint the backdrop white

Step 1: don't delete the cat.

Step2: Enter the code for the cat

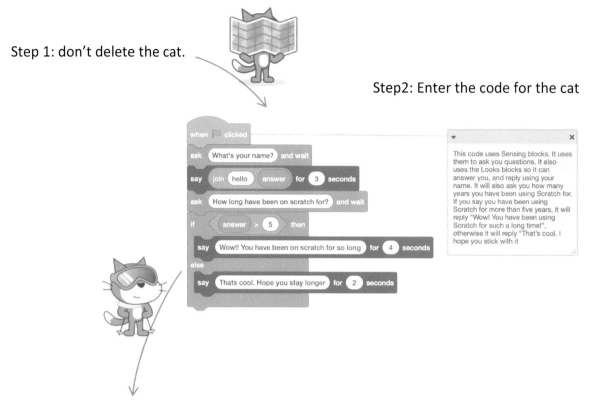

This code uses Sensing blocks. It uses them to ask you questions. It also uses the Looks blocks so it can answer you, and reply using your name. It will also ask you how many years you have been using Scratch for. If you say you have been using Scratch for more than five years, it will reply "Wow! You have been using Scratch for such a long time!", otherwise it will reply "That's cool. I hope you stick with it

Sensing blocks- Try adding more Sensing blocks!!!

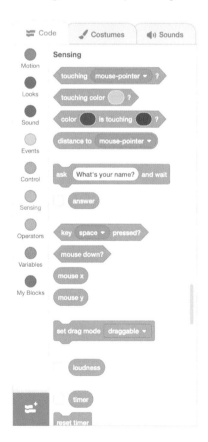

Now you have finished making the Question Asker 2 project.

PROJECT INTRODUCTION/RULES

You probably have played tip/tag or hide and seek. This is the digital version. The cat will be hiding somewhere, and you have to click on it with the mouse pointer if it pops up. If you succeed in clicking on it, you get a point.

Sprites	Backdrop
Cat1	canyon

Step1: don't delete the cat.

Step2: Enter the code for the cat

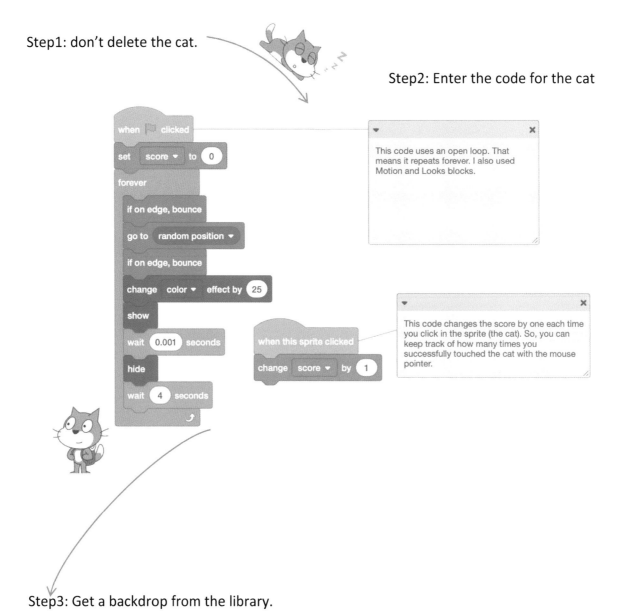

This code uses an open loop. That means it repeats forever. I also used Motion and Looks blocks.

This code changes the score by one each time you click in the sprite (the cat). So, you can keep track of how many times you successfully touched the cat with the mouse pointer.

Step3: Get a backdrop from the library.

canyon

You have now finished making the Hide and Seek 2 project.

PROJECT INTRODUCTION/RULES

Fidget spinners were very popular. Have you ever thought about a digital fidget spinner? You have to click the right arrow key to make it spin to the right, and the left arrow key to spin to the left. The fastest speed is 50.

Sprites	Backdrops
	Paint the backdrop white

Step 1: delete the cat, go to a new tab and search for "fidget spinner".

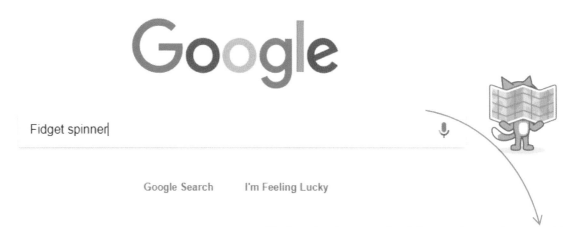

Find a nice image of a fidget spinner that you like.

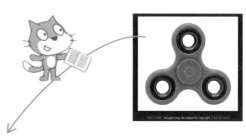

Step2: right click on the image and save it to your local computer.

Step3: Go back to your Scratch project and click on the button above

the Surprise button and then Upload Sprite to create a new sprite.

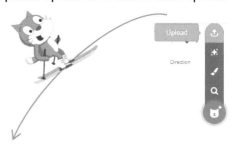

Select the file containing the image fidget spinner.

Step4: You now should have the fidget spinner sprite set up. Now enter the code for the sprite

Even more code!!!

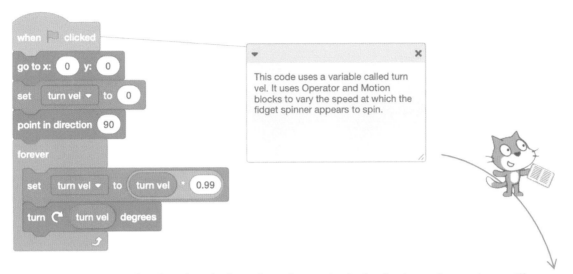

This code uses a variable called turn vel. It uses Operator and Motion blocks to vary the speed at which the fidget spinner appears to spin.

If you do the other bocks of code first, but do not include the last, the project will not run when you click on the green flag. The last block of code is the most important one. Try adding more fidget spinners, like these below!!!

Now you have finished making the Fidget Spinner project.

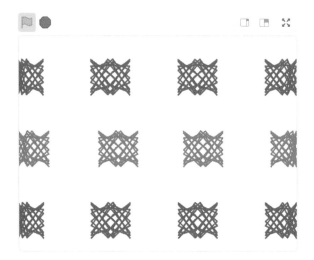

PROJECT INTRODUCTION/RULES

This is an art project, where you can turn the boxes into stars, and then turn the stars back into boxes.

Sprite	Backdrops
Create a sprite but leave it blank	Paint the backdrop White

Step1: Delete the cat and make a new sprite, but don't put anything in it

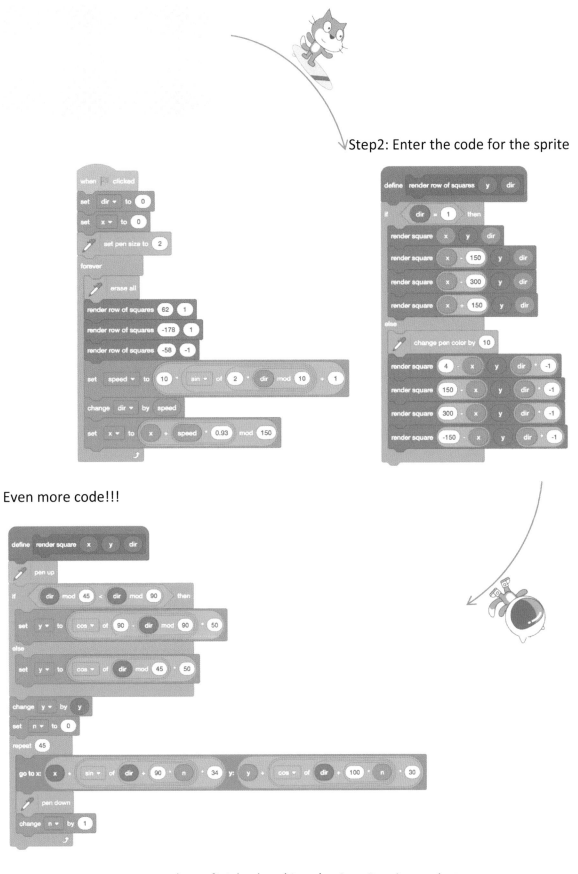

Step2: Enter the code for the sprite

Even more code!!!

Now you have finished making the Star Box Art project

Congratulations!!!, You have officially become an Expert programmer in scratch, but before we can go further, with the Expert projects, we have to first have a test! Complete the test and check your answers which are in the back of the book.

WHAT ARE THE NEW BLOCKS YOU HAVE LEARNT?

_____

WHAT ARE THE USES OF VARIABLES?

_____

HOW MANY TYPES OF VARIABLE ARE THERE?

_____

HOW DO YOU IMPORT IMAGES?

_____

HOW MANY PROJECTS CAN YOU MAKE WITH ONE ACCOUNT?

_____

IF YOU PUT 2 SONGS TOGETHER WILL THE SCRATCH SONG LAG?   (CIRCLE YOUR ANSWER)

Yes   No

WHAT IS THE BACKGROUND CALLED IN SCRATCH?

_____

AN ALGORITHM IS….

_____

WHAT IS THE DIFFERENCE BETWEEN SCRATCH 2.0 AND SCRATCH 3.0?

_____

CAN YOU EDIT YOUR SPRITE? (CIRCLE YOUR ANSWER)

Yes   No

MAKE A PROJECT WHERE A PERSON IS SICK AND THERE IS EQUIPMENT TO HELP HIM.

- Include a Human and a bed

YOU HAVE TO MAKE A CAR GAME WHERE IT HAS TO AVOID THE OBSTACLES.

- Include cars and some obstacles

YOU HAVE TO MAKE A PROJECT WHICH TEACHES STUDENTS HOW TO LIVE A HAPPIER LIFE.

- Use a teacher and some students with a classroom Backdrop

YOU HAVE TO MAKE A PROJECT WHICH GENERATES A DIAMOND SHAPE BY PEN.

- Use the pen from the extension area

ANSWERS

1) Operators

2) They can store data and information

3) There are four types of variable

4) You right click on the image you want then click save as. Save it to your local computer then go back to your project and click import.

5) As many as you want.

6) Yes

7) Backdrop

8) An algorithm is a computer procedure that tells your computer the steps required to solve a problem or to reach its goal.

9) The difference between 2.0 and 3.0 is that 3.0 with much neater and easier to see the blocks and drag them around.
10) Yes

Krish Nair from Cherrybrook Technology High School has been with iCodeNext as a L&D trainer; from an early age, bringing fun innovative ideas for projects and product testing for Scratch Coding courses and Text Coding. iCodeNext is a coding academy which teaches children coding and programming from age groups (5yr-12yrs). Although only 14 years old, Krish brings an immense knowledge base not only in the field of coding but also in the field of robotics and video creation and editing. Krish is a hands on person who loves to build and design creative projects and also design and write curriculum for budding coders. Krish has participated in many competitions such as the ANSTO Competition in 2017, Big ideas ANSTO 2020 and the upcoming Scinema International Science Film Feb 2021.

Printed in Great Britain
by Amazon